A Year of Yearning

A 12-Month Devotional to Help You Study God's Word More

Tricia K. Brown

Tricia K. Brown, The Girls Get Together
thegirlsgettogether.com

Copyright © 2020 Tricia K. Brown, The Girls Get Together   ISBN: 9798574129005

All rights reserved. Written permission must be secured from the publisher to use or reproduce any part of this book except for brief quotations in critical reviews or articles.

Scripture quotations marked (NIV) are taken from the Holy Bible, New International Version®, NIV®. Copyright © 1973, 1978, 1984, 2011 by Biblica, Inc.™ Used by permission of Zondervan. All rights reserved worldwide. www.zondervan.com The "NIV" and "New International Version" are trademarks registered in the United States Patent and Trademark Office by Biblica, Inc.™

Unless otherwise indicated, all Scripture quotations are taken from the Holy Bible, New Living Translation, copyright © 1996, 2004, 2007 by Tyndale House Foundation. Used by permission of Tyndale House Publishers, Inc., Carol Stream, IL 60188. All rights reserved.

Printed in the United States of America.

Contents

Title Page	1
Copyright	2
Yearning	9
Introduction	12
January	17
January Week One	18
Training Yourself in Godliness	19
January Week Two	22
Dining on God's Word	23
January Week Three	26
Giving Generously to Steward Well	27
January Week Four	31
Cleaning Up Your Spiritual Life	32
February	35
February Week One	36
Love is Kind	37
February Week Two	39
Love is Hopeful	40
February Week Three	42
Love is Patient	43

February Week Four	45
God is Love	46
March	49
March Week One	50
Grow in Prayer	51
March Week Two	54
Grow in Truth	55
March Week Three	58
Grow in Gratitude	59
March Week Four	62
Grow in Wisdom	63
April	67
April Week One	68
What We Can Learn from Malchus with the Missing Ear	69
April Week Two	72
What We Can Learn from the Boy in the Buff	73
April Week Three	77
What we can learn from Bad Guy Barabbas	78
April Week Four	81
What we can learn from Sight-Seeing Simon	82
May	85
May Week One	86
Being Thankful in Prayer	87
May Week Two	90
Interceding in Prayer	91
May Week Three	95
Praising in Prayer	96
May Week Four	100

Why Confession Counts	101
May Week Five	104
Being Silent in Prayer	105
June	109
June Week One	110
Why Christians Should Remain Self-Controlled	111
June Week Two	115
What to Do When You Are Afraid	116
June Week Three	120
Things to Remember When Grief's Got You Down	121
June Week Four	124
A Juxtaposition of Jealousy and Why It Matters	125
July	129
July Week One	130
Free from Sin and Death	131
July Week Two	134
Free to Live Well with God	135
July Week Three	138
Free to Live Well with Ourselves	139
July Week Four	142
Free to Live Well with Others	143
August	147
August Week One	148
The Problem of Sin and What We Can Do About It	149
August Week Two	154
What Does It Mean to Be Saved?	155
August Week Three	159
Angels Aren't Really in the Outfield—or Are They?	160

August Week Four	165
Ten Things You May Not Know About Heaven	166
August Week Five	171
The Alternative to Heaven is Hell—Not Somewhere You Want to Go	172
September	177
September Week One	178
Relying on God's Provision	179
September Week Two	183
Relying on God's Protection	184
September Week Three	189
Relying on God for Peace	190
September Week Four	195
Relying on God for Posterity	196
October	201
October Week One	202
What We Learn from the Boy Who Fell Out of the Window	203
October Week Two	208
What Falling Walls Can Teach Us About Faith	209
October Week Three	213
What Happened When the Ax Fell in the Water	214
October Week Four	218
What We Can Learn When a False god Falls Down	219
November	223
November Week One	224
Thoughts and Thankfulness	225
November Week Two	228
Learning to Be Content	229

November Week Three	232
Treating Others Well	233
November Week Four	235
More than Just Saying Thanks	236
December	239
December Week One	240
How to Find Favor When the News Is Unfavorable (Mary)	241
December Week Two	244
How to React When Your Plans are Revised (Joseph)	245
December Week Three	249
What God Expects After You Encounter Immanuel	250
December Week Four	254
What to Do When You Are Looking for Answers (Wisemen)	255
December Week Five	259
What to Do When You Can't Go Back	260
The Romans Road to Salvation	264
A Personal Note	265
Bibliography	266
Acknowledgements	267
About The Author	269
Connect with Tricia K. Brown	271

Yearning
a feeling of intense longing for something or someone

> *"My soul yearns, even faints,*
> *for the courts of the Lord;*
> *my heart and my flesh cry out*
> *for the living God."*
> PSALM 84:2 (NIV)

Dear Reader,

We all experience moments in time that are unforgettable, the "remember when" moments of our lives that define starting points, ending points, points of awakening or transition. Some of these moments are very public. Where were you when you heard the news of President Kennedy's assassination or Elvis Presley or Princess Diana's deaths? What were you doing when the Twin Towers fell? Do you remember watching the footage of the Newton school shootings? Those types of moments are often stunning, eye-opening, even scary.

However, it's usually the more personal moments that change the course of our lives. The moment we give our hearts to the Lord. The moment we say "I do." The moment we hold our child for the first time. The moment we hear the diagnosis. The moment we say good-bye.

On September 18, 2018, my twenty-year-old son, Brandon, died, and my life became forever divided between the "before" and "after" of that day.

During the darkness of the immediate aftermath of Brandon's death, I felt God's voice so clearly that it seemed almost audible, His whispering, "You are loved." I recited to myself often, "I love my God, and my God loves me" because, let's be honest, nothing about losing a 20-year-old seems very loving. I think God knew I needed the reassurance of His voice, His presence, even more profoundly than I ever had before. I also think that my utter and complete brokenness allowed me to be more fully present to God in a way that I had never before.

As I struggled through a fog of overwhelming grief, I found comfort in studying and sharing God's Word and how God uses the everyday experiences of my life to point me to Him. This book is a culmination of the devotions that I wrote and sent to my email subscribers that first year after my son died, a year in which my soul longed for God in new, unimaginable, and even painful ways.

I yearned for God to fix things. I yearned for God to turn back time. I yearned for God to bring back my son. I yearned for God to comfort me and my family. I yearned for God to help me understand. I yearned for God to take me Home so that I wouldn't have to feel the grief anymore. I yearned to know God more, to understand God better, to feel God more deeply, and to be with God in ways that I have never felt before. Perhaps, more than anything, Brandon's death has driven me to a deeper discontentment with this world and a greater desire for Heaven.

This is not a study on grief or sorrow or losing someone you love, but this book is a product of my grief and the lessons that God taught me during those first twelve months after my life changed forever. They are lessons that cover all aspects of life and walking with the Lord. They are lessons that I am still learning.

Life goes on, even when a part of your heart has died. I still seek to enjoy the life that God has given me, and I hope and pray that I will never lose the desire that He has placed in my soul, the yearning to grow in my relationship with Him. It's my hope that, in some small way, this book helps ignite a similar yearning in you.

With love and prayers,

Tricia K. Brown

Introduction

This is not a traditional women's devotional book. It's also not an in-depth Bible study either. It is something in between. If you're wondering then whether this book is for you, let me help you out.

- This book is for the woman who grew up in church but still gets a little confused by some of the religious terms the pastor uses on Sunday.
- This book is for the woman who sits in a pew every Sunday morning questioning whether or not she really has a "personal relationship" with Christ.
- It's for the woman who is a new Christian and wants to read the Bible but is a little intimidated.
- It's for the woman who has heard about Jesus but doesn't really know Who He is.
- This book is for mature Christians who want to dig deeper into matters of faith and scripture but just aren't sure where to start.
- It's also for the woman who is looking for something to share with the small group she leads.

This book is for you! However, it's not a quick fix. It's not a plan to read the Bible in a year. It's not a self-help or "how-to." Instead, this book includes life-tales and lessons that are meant to encourage you to open your Bible and read and pray and learn for yourself. These lessons are a starting point, a place to pique your curiosity and point you in the right direction. This book will not answer all your questions. It may even cause you to ask a few more. It will, however, steer you towards the place where you can discover all the solutions you need—God's Word.

Therefore, if you choose only to read this book, you may gain something from it, but you will miss out on the greatest blessing—reading God's Word for yourself. **My words are NOT God's words.** While I seek to share, teach, and inspire, my words should never replace God's Word in your life. If you have to choose between reading the Bible and this book, choose the Bible every time. However, if you are going to read this book (and I really hope you are), then here are a few suggestions on how to get the most out of it.

Find a Bible that you can read and understand. We all come from different educational backgrounds and have different intellectual abilities, but God's Word is written for all of us. God has a message for you, and He wants you to hear it. I personally use several translations when I study, but my favorite is the New Living Translation (NLT). If you have trouble reading, I would suggest finding an easy-to-read version. If you really have trouble reading, consider an audio Bible in the NLT or New International Version (NIV) or even a children's version of the Bible. There is no shame in finding a version you can read. God wants you to understand His Word.

Always begin your time in prayer. In Matthew 7:7-8, God says that if we seek, we will find. If we ask, it will be given. I don't see the need to repeat this in every lesson, but I sincerely hope you remember to do it. Begin your time with God by asking for His presence. Ask Him to help you understand what you are about to read and to show you how to apply it to your life.

Make it a practice to read God's Word every day. Sometimes we get so caught up in quantity that we lose track of quality. Bible study is not a race. The Bible can be hard to understand. Our human minds are limited in how much we can take in at any given time. Therefore, there is only one lesson for each of the four weeks in a month. This isn't to suggest that you should study God's Word only one day each week. The lesson should just be a starting point. Start the week by reading the lesson (what I've written) and the suggested Bible passages.

Then reread the suggested scripture passages every day, or (for longer passages), read a small portion of it every day until you complete it. You can also look up and read the other verses that are quoted or referenced in the lesson. If the lesson particularly spurs your interest, dive in and do some Biblical research of your own. By reading and re-reading scripture, you allow yourself the opportunity to soak up the words and give God time to speak to you personally.

Consider memorizing each week's memory verse. In Psalm 119:11, the psalmist talks about hiding God's Word in his heart so that he won't sin against God. It's good advice. Write each week's verse on a card and keep it nearby, repeating it frequently throughout the week. Keep your cards and periodically refresh your memory by reading them throughout the year.

Use what's given here to help you grow. Pay attention to the details in this book. Each series of lessons begins with the month and title of the series. Each lesson includes a page that gives the week number, the title of the lesson, what scriptures need to be read, the primary point of the lesson, and the memory verse. The titles and lessons are designed to help you think more about the scriptural theme, what God is saying to you, and how you can apply the scriptures to your life. The primary point is a "sticky statement" to help you remember the main focus of the lesson. At the end of each lesson is a blank space to write down your own thoughts and questions. This study will not answer all your questions, but asking them is a way to begin. Pray over your questions. You may be surprised when and where God provides an answer. In addition, email Tricia.Brown@thegirlsgettogether.com to receive a free scripture chart to download and print. This chart includes all the topics, scriptures, and memory verses included in the book, and will give you a handy tool to keep track of the scriptures you have read and memorized.

Start anywhere you want. This book is designed to have one theme per month, but you can start anytime of the year.

You can start at the beginning, or you can find the corresponding month you are in, start there, and circle back later. Each month's lessons stand alone. There are at least four lessons for each month, one for each week. If a month has five weeks but only four lessons, I encourage you to spend each day of the final week re-reading the scripture passage from the previous weeks' lessons. When there is a fifth week's lesson included and the month only has four weeks in it, I would encourage you to spend one weekend reading and studying the scriptures for that final lesson.

Reach out. If you haven't already, please visit thegirlsgettogether.com and sign up to receive my free devotional emails. Also, feel free to email me at tricia.brown@thegirlsgettogether.com with any questions, thoughts, comments, or feedback. I am so glad that you have allowed me to be a part of your spiritual journey. I would love to hear from you.

Studying God's Word can be hard. It's hard to find time, hard to be consistent, sometimes hard to understand. This year, I hope that you make the study of God's Word a priority in your life every day. So, what are you waiting for? I'm praying for you, and God wants to speak to you! Get started. It's time to dig in.

January

Resolutions that Really Matter

January Week One

Training Yourself in Godliness

Read: 1 Timothy 4:6-16

Primary Point: Commit to be spiritually fit; train for godliness.

Memory Verse: "Physical training is good, but training for godliness is much better, promising benefits in this life and in the life to come." *1 Timothy 4:8*

Training Yourself in Godliness

How many of you made resolutions? I love them. In fact, there are several on my list that rotate off one year and right onto the next. I bet you can guess which ones. I want to eat better, lose weight, and exercise more. Sound familiar? They are three of the top resolutions for many Americans. While there have been many unsuccessful years in the resolution department, 2017 turned out to be a game changer for me.

I have never exercised much, and, honestly, I hate it. I'm just not that kind of girl! Sweat and pain are not attractive to me in the least. In an effort to be healthier, I once again resolved to exercise regularly. I began riding a stationary bike 15 minutes a day on one of the lowest settings and increased it by 5 minutes each week until I reached a little over an hour a day on a "medium to high" setting. After a year and a half, I logged more than 3,000 miles. I was so proud; I told my boys I deserved a trophy.

Of course, exercise really is important, but the Bible tells us in 1 Timothy 4:8 that there is something much more important—training to be godly. Being godly is an odd kind of phrase if you really think about it. If we are godly, then we are, in essence, "like god," and we all know that's impossible. That's why we have to train! We have to train ourselves to recognize God's authority in our lives and, as a result of that recognition, endeavor to honor Him by the way we live.

Here's the problem. Training for anything is a multi-step process, and when it comes to spirituality, most of us stop with the first step. Just like I started out riding my bike for a small amount of time at a slow speed and slowly progressed as I grew stronger, we, as Christians, must seek to grow in our godliness. We must seek to improve. We must work at honoring Him by the way we live.

Now, don't get me wrong here. I am not saying that we work to earn our salvation. Salvation is a free gift of God (Ephesians 2:8). We don't work to earn our salvation, but we do work <u>as a result</u> of our salvation. Think of it this way. A runner doesn't work to sign up for a marathon, but once he signs up for a marathon, he trains so that he will be able to complete the marathon well. Once we are saved, we should want to train ourselves in godliness.

Unfortunately, that doesn't usually make the top ten popular resolutions for Americans. In fact, it doesn't even make the cut for many Christians, but it should. It's important. It's more important than our health and beauty goals, our financial goals, or even our career goals. If you are a Christian, then one of your daily resolutions should be to train yourself to be more like God. You can start by praying regularly and reading our training manual, the Bible. The book of Proverbs, for example, offers lots of practical suggestions on where to begin.

- The godly love the truth. (Proverbs 13:5)
- The godly are generous. (Proverbs 11:25)
- The godly are honest. (Proverbs 11:5)
- The godly are just. (Proverbs 12:5)
- The godly care for the poor. (Proverbs 29:7)
- The godly care for animals. (Proverbs 12:10)
- The godly give wise advice. (Proverbs 12:26)

That gives me plenty to work on, but, if you have all those mastered, there's plenty more.

In 1 Timothy 4:12(b), Paul reminds us to be a good example "in the way you live, in your love, your faith, and your purity." That encompasses just about everything.

Face it. Training is hard work. Physical training requires effort, and so does spiritual training. The Bible tells us that training for godliness is valuable because it will benefit us not only in this present life but also in eternity. While the rewards of physical exercise may be worth the effort, the results of growing more godly are even more so.

Notes:

January Week Two

Dining on God's Word

Read: Matthew 4:1-11

Primary Point: For spiritual power, feed on God's Word.

Memory Verse: "But Jesus told him, 'No! The Scriptures say, 'People do not live by bread alone, but by every word that comes from the mouth of God.'" *Matthew 4:4*

Dining on God's Word

Perhaps you have seen the meme that says, "My idea of a balanced diet is having chocolate in both hands." I so relate. Eating less and eating healthy (or healthier) is always one of the top resolutions on my list. What about you?

While watching our diets is definitely a good thing, the Bible tells us that the most important nourishment we receive is actually spiritual nourishment, and that comes from the Word of God. By looking at the story of Christ's temptation in the wilderness, we learn about the importance of hiding God's Word in our hearts.

Knowing God's Word Gives You A Response To Temptation.

Jesus was hungry. He hadn't eaten in 40 days. Most of us can't imagine fasting 24 hours, let alone 40 days. If we miss a meal, we think we're starving. When Satan tempted Jesus to turn the stones into bread, it was a real temptation. Jesus was obviously hungry, and He had the power to do something about it, but Jesus didn't have to prove Himself to Satan or to anyone else. How did He combat Satan's enticements? With the Word of God. Jesus quoted a portion of Deuteronomy 8:2-3, reminding Satan (and us) that there are some things more important than food.

Temptations are Satan's way of attacking our defenses. He wants us to lower our guard and do things that will draw us away from God and cause harm to ourselves. Ephesians 6:17 reminds us that scripture is our weapon of defense. When we are faced with circumstances or choices that are inviting us to sin, we can wield God's Word to defend ourselves.

Knowing God's Word Helps You Discern Truth.

In the best of lies, there is a little bit of truth. Even Satan knows this. When it came to the second way in which he tried to tempt Jesus, he chose to incorporate a selection from Psalms 91 to persuade Jesus to demonstrate His power. There is more to knowing God's Word than just quoting words off the page. Jesus was quick to point out the contradiction (and therefore untruth) that Satan presented in his temptation. Using Deuteronomy 6:16, Jesus refuted Satan's attempt by pointing out that God's Word clearly directs no one to tempt God. This was not only an indictment of Satan's attempt to tempt the Lord but also an explanation of why it would be wrong for Jesus to concede to the request.

Hebrews 4:12 tells us that God's Word is "sharper than a two-edged sword." Since Satan is crafty and will use every means available to draw us off the right path, it is imperative that we actually know and understand God's Word. By doing so, we will be able to discern between what is the truth and what is a lie.

Knowing God's Word Leads You To Triumph.

Three strikes, and you're out. Satan tried three times to tempt Jesus, and all three times, Jesus countered with the Word of God. In the end, Jesus's final words to Satan were from Deuteronomy 6:13, reminding Satan of God's superiority. Satan left, defeated.

Psalm 119:11 tells us that we should hide God's Word in our heart so that we won't sin against Him. While we strive to watch what we put in our mouths, we need to pay as much (if not more) attention to what we are putting into our hearts and minds. For spiritual power, feed on God's Word.

Notes:

January Week Three

Giving Generously to Steward Well

Read: Luke 10:30-37

Primary Point: Don't be greedy; give generously.

Memory Verse: "Tell them to use their money to do good. They should be rich in good works and generous to those in need, always being ready to share with others." *1 Timothy 6:18*

Giving Generously to Steward Well

The beginning of the year often brings financial goals. Some people want to get out of debt. Some people want to save more. Some people just want to learn to manage their money better. The Bible has a lot to say about money. Some reports indicate that money is, in fact, mentioned over 2,000 times in the Bible. I haven't counted. One thing I can be certain about is this. God is more concerned with our heart than He is with our pocketbooks.

The Good Samaritan is a fairly common Bible story. Even many non-religious people know the gist of the story. The term itself has become synonymous with a person who helps someone in need. This passage in Luke has been used to illustrate sermons on a wide variety of topics including the dangers of hypocrisy, the ills of discrimination, and the value of compassion. It's true that all of those lessons can easily be discovered within the seven verses that relay this short story. First and foremost, though, the good Samaritan is a story of generosity.

Interestingly, being generous is not the same as giving. A person can give but not give generously. Being generous means to give more than is necessary or expected. In addition, generosity is not limited to financial giving. The Good Samaritan offers key insights into how we, as believers, can be better stewards of all the resources God has given us. First, let's consider what, exactly, the Samaritan gave.

He Gave His Time And Attention.

Have you ever wondered what the Samaritan was doing that day on the road that ran between Jerusalem and Jericho? The road was between 15 and 18 miles long, was a particularly arduous hike, and offered little opportunity for shade or water. While it was a frequent route for merchants and travelers, it was also a notorious place for bandits. It definitely wasn't the kind of road that you would take for a leisurely walk. So, we can safely assume that the Samaritan was going somewhere for some reason. He had things to do, people to see, and places to go. Yet, when he saw the injured Jewish man, he stopped. He didn't just stop to peruse the situation, like we often do as we drive slowly by the scene of a car accident. He went out of his way. He took a detour. He went "over to him." When he got there, he didn't try to flag down other travelers who may have been passing by. He didn't tell the man that he was going to send help soon. He didn't slap a band-on on his boo-boos and wish him well. He spent time with the man. He took care of him. He didn't rush, and he didn't try to find a quick way out.

He Gave His Comfort And Security.

We usually skip right over this part of the story. We're impressed enough that the man stopped to help, but we fail to think about what it cost him in terms of comfort. The Samaritan had a donkey, but when he picked up the ailing traveler, there likely wasn't room for two. Guess who had to walk? Since the Bible tells us that he took care of the man after having arrived at an inn, we can surmise that the Samaritan probably didn't get much sleep that night either. The Samaritan sacrificed more than just physical comfort.

The Bible calls him "a despised Samaritan." Why was he despised? Samaritans were considered half-breeds, a result of

Israelites who had, generations before, bred with Assyrians. Samaritans were hated by most Jewish people, and most of the time, the feeling was mutual for the Samaritans as well. Had the roles been reversed, it is very likely that the Jewish traveler would have left the Samaritan to die. In caring for a Jew, the Samaritan sacrificed not only his time and money but also his pride.

In addition, we have to remember, that while the Samaritan was taking the time to care for the injured man on the side of the road, he was in fact, making himself a target of the very bandits that had beaten and robbed the Jew. If the bandits didn't get him, there was the very real danger that another Jew might misinterpret the situation, and attack the Samaritan. The Samaritan set aside his pride, prejudices, comfort, and security because he felt compassion for this person in need.

He Gave His Skill And Resources.

Giving from our resources is often the easiest way for us to give. Sometimes, in fact, it is very easy for us to simply throw money at a problem. Notice all the things the Samaritan did before he actually gave money. First, he gave his olive oil (used for healing) and some sort of cloth to help bandage his wounds. He also gave the man wine to help quench his thirst and provide some means of pain management. These were his possessions, things that he most likely packed for himself, for his needs. Then, he gave them to a stranger.

Notice that he also gave his skill. He personally bandaged the man's wounds and tended to him through the night. He didn't just pay someone else; he did the dirty work. Finally, he paid for a room where he could rest and heal, not just for one night but for as many nights as were necessary. He gave of his material resources, his monetary resources, and his own skills to provide care for a complete stranger.

The Samaritan gave generously—above and beyond what was expected. We can learn a lot from him. How we manage our finances is very important, but learning to crunch numbers, set budgets, and squirrel away money is not all there is to becoming a good steward.

Proverbs 19:17 reminds us that those who are generous to the poor are lending to the Lord. 2 Corinthians 9:7 tells us that God loves a cheerful giver. 1 Timothy 6:17-19 commands us to be rich in good works, generous and ready to share.

As counterintuitive as it may seem, one of the first lessons we can learn when trying to govern our greenbacks is to give generously of our time, attention, comfort and security as well as our material and monetary possessions. It's often inconvenient, uncomfortable, and even exorbitant, but the Bible assures us in 2 Corinthians 9:6 that when we plant generously, we reap a generous crop. Let's plant well this year.

Notes:

January Week Four

Cleaning up Your Spiritual Life

Read: Luke 11:14-26

Primary Point: We can't just empty our lives of bad; we have to fill our lives with Good.

Memory Verse: "Anyone who isn't with me opposes me, and anyone who isn't working with me is actually working against me." *Luke 11:23*

Cleaning Up Your Spiritual Life

Something about a new year often brings a renewed desire to clean and organize our homes. Japanese organizational specialist, Marie Kondo, devised the now famous, "Does it spark joy?" method of decluttering. Basically, you are supposed to go through your things and get rid of anything that doesn't bring you joy.

I am a sucker for organization. In fact, I honestly think I could be an organization specialist. Although, I love to clean out and organize closets and drawers, there is something about Ms. Kondo's method that disturbs me. Depending on my mood, I could get rid of a lot of very necessary items in my house that don't necessarily bring me joy!

Still, decluttering is a good thing, especially for those of us who tend to accumulate too much. In fact, I think, for the majority of us, decluttering is a natural tendency that grows from a desire to simplify and better our lives.

Maybe that's why we often want to handle our spiritual lives in the same way. We think that by getting rid of enough sinful habits or "bad things" we can become better, more spiritual people. Luke 11:14-26 throws an interesting spin on this fallacy.

This passage about unclean spirits and clean houses seems a little "out there," not something that has any practical application for our lives, right?

Wrong.

These verses offer a surprising bit of advice for us. Just like the man in this parable, we often try to get rid of the "unclean" things in our lives. We try to dispose of our dirty secrets, sweep away our sinful habits, and tidy up after our transgressions. We stop drinking alcohol, flirting with someone other than our spouse, looking at unwholesome images, cursing like a sailor, and losing our patience with the gal talking on her phone while driving very slowly in the fast lane. We try to make ourselves better.

Through this story, Jesus reminds us that just getting rid of the bad isn't enough. A clean but empty life is still a life that is open to Satan's attacks in even greater proportions. **We can't just empty our lives of everything bad; we have to fill our lives with something good.**

If you aren't a believer, the first step is coming to the Lord and accepting Him as your Savior so that you can be filled with the Holy Spirit. Even if you were able to get rid of everything bad in your life (which you aren't), you can't earn your salvation by doing so (Ephesians 2:8). You need God's grace and His gracious gift of the Holy Spirit to fill your heart and life. Once a believer, the next step is to fill your life with the fruits of the Spirit: love, joy, peace, patience, kindness, goodness, faithfulness, gentleness, and self-control (Galatians 5:22).

In 1 Corinthians 6:19-20, Paul reminds believers that their bodies are temples of the Holy Spirit and tells them to glorify God in their bodies. Ephesians 4:21-24 tells us, "Since you have heard about Jesus and have learned the truth that comes from him, throw off your old sinful nature and your former way of life, which is corrupted by lust and deception. Instead, let the Spirit renew your thoughts and attitudes. Put on your new nature, created to be like God—truly righteous and holy."

It's not enough to just get rid of the old life; we have to put on the new. If we are getting rid of filthy talk, we need to replace it with encouraging, loving, words (1 Thessalonians 5:11). If we are emptying ourselves of selfishness, we need to become more generous (2 Corinthians 9:7). If we clean out immoral thoughts, we need to think on things that are excellent and worthy of praise (Philippians 4:8). If we trash our unkind ways, we need instead to display kindness and mercy (Colossians 3:12).

Newton's third law of motion states that every action has an equal and opposite reaction. The opposite of emptying is filling. Parents everywhere can relate. We clean out a child's room. We can see the floor. There is space in the closet. There are maybe even a few dresser drawers empty, and then, a week later, things are falling out on top of you when you open the closet. The dresser drawers are crammed full, and you are tripping over things as you try to walk through the room. Empty spaces tend to fill up, and often the second filling proves even worse than the original. Unless you submit to the Lord's authority and guidance and allow His Spirit to move in, your efforts to clean up will be worthless in the end.

So, while you're tossing out broken toys and taking unused clothes to Goodwill, think about your spiritual clean-up as well. Remember, when it comes to our life with Christ, we can't just declutter, we have to also redecorate.

Notes:

February

What is Love?

February Week One

Love is Kind

Read: 1 Corinthians 13 and 2 Samuel 9

Primary Point: One key to loving well is to just be kind.

Memory Verse: "Love is patient and kind. Love is not jealous or boastful or proud." *1 Corinthians 13:4*

Love is Kind

Can you imagine being friends with someone whose father wanted to kill you? That was the predicament in which David found himself (1 Samuel 20).

He and Jonathan were pals, buddies, the best of friends, like brothers. Jonathan's father, King Saul, wanted to kill David. Jonathan wanted to believe the best of his dad, but the evidence was undeniable. When push came to shove, Jonathan knew it was true. King Saul wanted to destroy David.

David was God's anointed. David was destined to take King Saul's place, and that meant that Jonathan would not inherit the throne. Given the circumstances, we might understand if Jonathan had chosen to side with his dad, but he didn't. He was loyal to his friend and helped him escape his father's wrath. All he asked for in return was David's kindness. Jonathan wanted David to be kind to him and his family when David came to the throne, in spite of the grief that his father would inflict.

David agreed, and, years later he remembered his promise. When the dust settled and the kingdom was finally his, King David searched out and found Jonathan's remaining heir and was indeed very kind to him.

The dictionary defines kindness as being friendly, generous, considerate. It isn't really that hard. Or is it? Most of the time it's easy to be kind to people who are kind to us. Sometimes it's easy to be kind to people we like. But what about strangers? What about people who take us for granted? What about people who hurt us or use us? What about our enemies? Kindness isn't always easy.

John 13:35 tells us that the world will know we are Christians by our love, and love is kind. What does kindness look like on a practical level? It's answering softly when you feel like yelling. It's giving more when you feel like you have nothing left to give. It's thinking about others when you feel left out. It's listening even when you're in a hurry. It's thinking of others more than yourself. Kindness is usually about the small things.

Years ago, as a harried mom of four little boys, I made a trip to Kroger one day to do a little grocery shopping while I had a minute alone. I don't remember who watched my boys or even where they were. I don't remember what I was buying or what my plans were for the rest of the day. I do remember this. I felt tired, worn-down, and unattractive. I also remember what I was wearing because a woman came up to me and said, "I love your headband and shirt. It matches so nicely." I was wearing a green headband and a green shirt. There was absolutely nothing special about the outfit. Green is actually my least favorite color, and if I had my hair pulled back in a headband, it probably meant I spent very little time fixing it. Yet, a stranger complimented me, and years later, I still remember her words. Why? Because she made me smile. She made me think a little better of myself. She made me feel good.

Jonathan was kind to David. David was kind to Jonathan, not only when it was convenient, but also when it was difficult, dangerous, and daring, even when there was nothing to be gained in return.

You never know the power of one small act of kindness. So, be kind today... love.

Notes:

February Week Two

Love is Hopeful

Read: 1 Corinthians 13 and 1 Samuel 1

Primary Point: Hopeful love is not only a confident expectation but also a Godly pursuit of good things.

Memory Verse: "Love never gives up, never loses faith, is always hopeful, and endures through every circumstance." *1 Corinthians 13:7*

Love is Hopeful

Hannah prayed for a child. She promised that if God gave her one, she would give him back to God. God answered and gave her a son. Can you imagine the temptation she must have felt to renege on that promise? I'm sure she came up with a hundred reasons why she shouldn't leave her little boy at the temple. Number one on the list was probably the fact that Eli, the priest, was not exactly stellar father material. Everyone knew about Eli's sons and the wicked things they were doing right under Eli's nose (1 Samuel 2:12-26). Surely God wouldn't expect Hannah to leave her precious child under the influence of such ungodly men. Surely, God would understand that Samuel needed his mom.

If Hannah had such doubts, she kept them to herself, because scripture records that she did just as she promised God she would do. In doing so, she gave us another example of love. When Hannah gave Samuel, the son for whom she had prayed, the son who she loved, her precious gift from God, back to the Lord from whom he came, she gave us a visible demonstration of the hopeful nature of love itself.

What is hope? Is hope a wish? Is hope a dream or a far-fetched desire? When the Bible tells us that love is patient, we understand what that means, even if it's difficult to carry out. When the Bible says that love is kind, we get it. We know how to show kindness, even if we don't always do it.

When the Bible says that love is hopeful, what does that mean? What is hope, and how can we put "hope" into action?

Hannah can help us understand. Hannah hoped when she asked the Lord for a child, and Hannah hoped while she waited to become pregnant. Hope, as it relates to love, is what Hannah demonstrated when she willingly left her son on the steps of the temple and went home alone. Hannah's love for Samuel was encompassed in hope that God Himself, and not Eli or his wicked sons, would raise Samuel; hope that Samuel would grow in the nurture and admonition of the Lord and become a Godly man and leader; hope that the child who she loved would be safe, sound, and happy even without the arms of a mother to hold him. Hannah's love was rooted in hope.

Hope is the expectation of something good. The Bible is full of verses that tell us things for which we can hope, but we don't usually think of "hope" as an action verb. At best, we think of it as an emotion, but like all of the other definitions of love in 1 Corinthians 13, hope does indeed carry with it a measure of activity. Hannah's hope was put into action by the surrender of her parental rights. In the same way, hopeful love involves exertion. We demonstrate hopeful love when we choose to exercise with a friend who is struggling with weight loss. We express hopeful love when we write notes of encouragement to our spouse who is frustrated with his job. We love with hope when we discipline our children in order to teach them obedience.

Biblical hope is not only a confident expectation but also a Godly pursuit of good things. While each individual is personally responsible for pursuing good, hopeful love is best demonstrated by helping others in those pursuits. How do we love like that? By tapping into the source, "God, the source of hope, (who) will fill you completely with joy and peace because you trust in Him" Romans 15:3. So, demonstrate hope... love.

Notes:

February Week Three

Love is Patient

Read: 1 Corinthians 13 and Genesis 29:13-30

Primary Point: It's not a pitter-patter of the heart, love is patient from the start.

Memory Verse: "Always be humble and gentle. Be patient with each other, making allowance for each other's faults because of your love." *Ephesians 4:2*

Love is Patient

Jacob was new in town, but he was fitting in quite well. He had a job, was working hard, and truly believed that the Lord would prosper him. It wasn't long before he met Rachel. She was beautiful, but she was also the boss's daughter. Jacob was smitten. He wanted to spend his life with her.

So, Jacob did something unexpected. During a wage negotiation, he summoned his courage and asked Laban for his daughter's hand in marriage. Laban agreed, but the bride price was seven years of Jacob's labor. Jacob complied and set about earning his bride.

Despite the hard labor, the time flew by. The days were spent working; evenings were spent taking long walks with Rachel, dreaming of their life ahead together, planning for a family.

Finally, the day came, and, according to custom, Rachel met Jacob hidden in her bridal attire. After the wedding ceremony, they were escorted in the dark to their new home where they consummated their marriage.

Rachel was quieter than usual, but Jacob hardly noticed. He was so excited to have his wife, to begin their future together. He knew that Rachel loved him and that she was just as excited to be together.

When morning came, and Jacob turned to look at his new bride's face, he was shocked to see that it wasn't his beloved Rachel at all. Jacob's father-in-law had, in fact, deceived him into marrying Rachel's older sister. Jacob was devastated and infuriated. Storming in to see the man, Jacob demanded an answer. Laban explained that in their culture, the oldest daughter should be married first. Of course, he agreed that Jacob could still marry Rachel, but Jacob would have to work another seven years, and Jacob did.

Despite prevailing popular opinion and consumer marketing, love is not a feeling. It has little to do with heart palpitations and flutters and even less to do with chocolates and flowers. According to 1 Corinthians 13, love is a series of actions, one of which is to be patient. Patience is being able to tolerate difficult circumstances or even provocation without responding negatively. Jacob's love for Rachel was patient.

What about our love?

Are we patient with our spouses when they leave their dirty clothes all over the bedroom floor? Are we patient with our children when they fight with their siblings? Are we patient with our friends when they fail to respond to our text messages?

In light of Jacob's sacrifice, these incidents seem petty, don't they? Yet, these are the kinds of ordinary grievances that try our patience every day. They also give us the opportunity to display love.

Colossians 3:12 says, "Since God chose you to be the holy people he loves, you must clothe yourselves with tenderhearted mercy, kindness, humility, gentleness, and patience."

Ephesians 4:2 says, "Be completely humble and gentle; be patient, bearing with one another in love."

We should bear with one another...
- when we are tired,
- when we are frustrated,
- when we disagree,
- when we don't get our way,
- when we are mistreated.

Be patient... love.

Notes:

February Week Four

God is love

Read: 1 Corinthians 13 and 1 John 4:7-21

Primary Point: When God lives in us, love should pour out of us.

Memory Verse: "Dear friends, let us continue to love one another, for love comes from God. Anyone who loves is a child of God and knows God. But anyone who does not love does not know God, for God is love."   *1 John 4:7-8*

God is Love

What is the greatest love story you ever heard? Maybe it is a fictional tale from a romantic novel. Maybe it's a life of loyalty and endearment that you witnessed between your grandma and grandpa. Maybe it's the sacrifice you've seen displayed between a husband and a wife or a parent and a child. Whatever love story has been written or lived, there is one greater than all. It's one that is known well but often taken for granted.

"For God so loved the world that He gave His only begotten son that whosoever believeth in Him should not perish but have everlasting life." John 3:16

What a love story that is!

God is patient. He waits for us. God is kind. He provides for us. God is hopeful. He grants promises to us. God loves. God loves us. What is love? Love is patient. Love is kind. Love is hopeful.

"God is love, and all who live in love live in God, and God lives in them." 1 John 4:16

While 1 Corinthians 13 gives us a breakdown of the actions that define love, 1 John 4 sums it up with a few stark commands. God is love, and we love each other because He first loved us. If we say that we love God but then hate someone else, we're lying. If we love God, we must love fellow believers. It's all pretty cut and dry. Love! Love! Love!

The problem is, people are hard to love. People (including you and me) are hard to love because we're imperfect creatures. We make mistakes. We hurt others, sometimes unintentionally but sometimes intentionally. We think more of ourselves than we do the people around us. It's hard for us to love each other.

Let's admit it. It's hard to love when our spouse betrays us. It's hard to love when our children defy us. It's hard to love when our friends ignore us. It's hard to love when our boss takes us for granted. Love is hard.

God says love. How can we do it? How can we really love? The key to loving is those three little words... "God is love."

If it's up to you and me, we'll never truly love, not in the way God wants us to love. Our patience, our kindness, our hopefulness are severely limited by our own human nature, our own self-centeredness. We can't put into practice all the actions that God commands us to do and not do in order to truly love others. We simply can't. It's not in us, unless of course, God is in us. When we are filled with God, we are then, in essence, filled with love, love in its truest sense. Then and only then, through the power of the Holy Spirit living in us, love will pour out of us and onto all the perfectly imperfect people we know.

So, as this month of love comes to a close, remember this. If you want to love like Jesus, you need more of Jesus in you. The more we love Him, the better we can love each other!

Notes:

March

A Time to Grow

March Week One

Grow in Prayer

Read: Colossians 1

Primary Point: Growth isn't just for plants; grow in prayer.

Memory Verse: "We also pray that you will be strengthened with all his glorious power so you will have all the endurance and patience you need. May you be filled with joy." *Colossians 1:11*

Grow in Prayer

Spring is just around the corner, or so we hope. When I look out from my back deck, I can see green shoots beginning to emerge, poking their heads out despite the frigid temperatures. Daffodils parade along the side of the roadway on my morning commute. It is March, and March is, after all, a time of growth.

Growth isn't just for plants. As Christians, we are called to grow in our spiritual walks as well. Colossians 1:10 says, "you will grow as you learn to know God better and better." Throughout the four short chapters of Colossians, we can learn specific ways that we can nourish our spiritual growth. Like adding fertilizer to your garden soil, the apostle Paul gives instructions to help spur us on towards spiritual maturity. One of the first things he addresses is how we can grow in prayer.

Pray Constantly

When Paul talks about prayer, he uses words like "always" and "we have not stopped." It's obvious that Paul was vigilant in his prayer life. He was in constant communication with the Lord. I would venture to say that most of us pray, and we may even pray frequently, but do we pray "always?" Do we pray constantly? If we want to grow in prayer, we need to be persistent and consistent. We need to spend time in devoted and specific prayer, but we also need to carry with us an attitude of prayer.

Remember, prayer is a conversation. Therefore, you should be ready to listen as God speaks to you in His still quiet voice throughout your day.

Pray With Contentment

Paul most likely wrote this epistle while he was under house arrest. Yet, he still expressed contentment and thanksgiving to God. So often we approach God with our list of requests. We fail to thank Him for all that He has already done. Imagine your children or your spouse coming to you to have a conversation. How would you feel if every conversation started with "Please give me..." or "Would you do this?" It would be frustrating, to say the least. We would feel underappreciated, not really loved. Still, that's the way we often treat God.

No matter what circumstances we face, there is always something for which we can be thankful. We should pray with joy, expressing our contentment with Who God is and what He has already given us. We should remember that He is God, and He deserves our praise and worship for that alone. It is important to be intentional in the time we spend with God and to make it more about Him and less about us.

Pray With Concern

This may seem easy at first. We know how to be concerned. We are concerned about our health and the health of our loved ones. We are concerned about finances, car repairs, the new job, or our kids' educations. There's nothing wrong with praying about all those things. In fact, God encourages us to "cast all our cares on Him" (1 Peter 5:7).

If you notice, though, Paul's concerns are a little deeper, a little less physical, and a lot more intellectual and spiritual. If we want to grow in prayer, we need to be more concerned about matters of eternity. Paul prayed for things like knowledge of God's will, spiritual wisdom and understanding, strength, endurance and patience, opportunities to speak about Christ, and the ability to proclaim the gospel clearly. Those are the types of things that need to top our prayer lists if we are to grow in the image of Christ.

Growing isn't easy. Spring plants have to push through the dirt, hardened and cold from the long winter. Growing takes time. Even though I can see green shoots, it will be many weeks, even months, before most of the plants in my garden bloom. Like those plants, growing is what we are meant to do. Paul encouraged the Colossians to grow, and he encourages us to as well. Let's start with our prayer life this week. Let's be constant, content, and most of all concerned, not only with matters of life, but even more so about our relationships with Christ. Grow in prayer.

Notes:

March Week Two

Grow in Truth

Read: Colossians 2

Primary Point: Take time to root yourself in truth.

Memory Verse: "And now, just as you accepted Christ Jesus as your Lord, you must continue to follow him. Let your roots grow down into him, and let your lives be built on him. Then your faith will grow strong in the truth you were taught, and you will overflow with thankfulness." *Colossians 2:6-7*

Grow in Truth

One day when my son, Brandon, was just a little fellow, he simply refused to eat his sandwich. I told him that it must be eaten and walked out of the room. Upon my hasty return, I noticed that Brandon's plate was empty. I realized that he could not have eaten a whole sandwich that quickly and asked him, "Where is your sandwich?"

"I ate it," he replied matter-of-factly.

Wanting to give him a chance to come clean, I asked again, "Brandon, you ate your sandwich?"

"Yes," he said.

Lying in our house is a very serious offense. So, once again, I asked in my most motherly voice, "Brandon, did you really eat all of your sandwich?"

"Yes," he said, unfazed.

I went to the trash can, opened the lid, and there, right on top, was the sandwich.

We laughed about the incident later, but that day, Brandon learned a lesson about telling the truth.

Many people today think that truth is relative. They believe there is no "black" and "white" when it comes to morality, only grim shades of gray.

The Bible tells us differently. "The very essence of your words is truth," the psalmist writes (Psalm 119:160) of God's

Word. We read in John 17:17, "Make them holy by your truth; teach them your word which is truth." In John 14:6, Jesus Himself declares, "I am the way, the truth, and the life…"

There is such a thing as truth. It is found only in and through God Himself, in His Word and through His Son. Let's look at four specific truths that Paul teaches us in this chapter.

Truth 1: We Are Confident In Christ.

Verse 2 tells us that as Christ followers we can have complete confidence. Confidence in what? In ourselves? In our circumstances? In the world around us? No, we can be confident of "God's mysterious plan, which is Christ Himself." We can be confident in the message of the cross, that Christ made a way for us to be redeemed through faith. We can be confident that our lives rest surely in His hands. Our confidence is found only in Christ.

Truth 2: We Are Complete With Christ.

Not only are we confident in Christ, we are also complete in Him (verse 10). We don't have to add anything to the gospel. No matter how good (or bad) we are, we can't do what only God has done. Our salvation is complete in Christ. Colossians 2:12-14 explains that we are forgiven and made alive by trusting in the "mighty power of God, who raised Christ from the dead." We are complete with Christ.

Truth 3: We Are Created New Because Of Christ.

Verse 11 talks about spiritual circumcision. When we place our faith in Christ, our sinful nature is cut away. We are given a "new life." Paul talks more about the kind of life we should be living in chapter 3. Let's just say, anything new should look differently from the old.

Truth 4: We Are Connected To Christ And Each Other.

In Colossians, we discover that as Christians we are not just followers of Christ. We are actually connected to Christ. Paul likens our relationship to Christ like a body. Christ is the head. He is our authority, our ruler. We are also "knit together" or connected to one another. As Christ holds us together, we are free to grow as God desires—closer to Him and to each other.

Confidant in Christ. Complete with Christ. Created new because of Christ. Connected to Christ and each other. Knowing and understanding these four things will anchor our roots and help our faith grow strong. That is the promise of Colossians. That is the truth.

Notes:

March Week Three

Grow in Gratitude

Read: Colossians 3

Primary Point: To live like Christ is to grow in gratitude.

Memory Verse: "And let the peace that comes from Christ rule in your hearts. For as members of one body you are called to live in peace. And always be thankful." *Colossians 3:15*

Grow in Gratitude

"Always be thankful." Have you ever thought about the seeming impossibility of that statement?
- What about when the policeman gives you a speeding ticket?
- What about when your child throws a monumental fit in the middle of church?
- What about when your spouse cheats?
- What about when the doctor gives a terrible diagnosis?
- What about when someone dies?

Always be thankful? Is that really what God means in this scripture? Is that even possible? Surely, there is a caveat.

God really does mean what He says. It is possible, and no, there is no caveat. Being thankful is another area where we are commanded to grow, but gratitude starts on a very basic level. In order to increase our capacity for thankfulness, the author of Colossians points out three areas we must first address.

Our Perspective

In order to be thankful, we have to think about "things of heaven." What does that mean? Are we to sit around and think about angels sitting on clouds playing harps? Are we to concentrate on streets of gold? While imagining what our eternal home will look like has some benefit, I don't think that's really what is being suggested.

Verse 11 tells us that "Christ is all that matters." So, setting our sights on Heaven is really all about setting our sights on Christ and looking at things from a Heavenly perspective. When a day doesn't go as planned, consider the misadventures in light of eternity. When we are angry, or frustrated, or hurt by others, we should remember all that Christ has done for us. When we receive bad news and our hearts are breaking, we must turn to our Savior for comfort, help, and hope. Does it mean that life will be easy? Of course not. Keeping our eyes on the finish line simply helps us endure the pain and be more thankful in the process.

Our Practices

Keeping the right perspective definitely plays a part in how grateful we are, but what we do and don't do is also important. Verses 5-9 of Colossians 3, list a whole litany of "don'ts." God gives us restrictions or boundaries for a few reasons. First, He wants us to glorify Him in the way we live. Second, He wants to keep us from things that will cause us harm. Third, He wants to lead us toward things that will bring us good. By avoiding "sinful, earthly things" like "sexual immorality, impurity, lust, and evil desires" (as well as all the other negatives listed in those verses), God is actually helping us to live in a way that sets us apart as Christ followers. When we live the "new life" described in this chapter, we will begin to develop hearts that are full of gratitude.

For example, when we avoid sexual immorality, we are all the more thankful for the Godly ways we are given to express sexuality in marriage. When we forsake greed, our hearts can learn contentment for the monetary blessings God brings our way. As we seek to avoid lies and deception, we develop a greater appreciation for truth.

In our efforts to put Godly practices into our lives, we will actually grow hearts that are full of gratitude and become more like Christ.

Our Partnerships

The majority of these verses actually center around this very important category. If we want to be thankful, we have to consider the partnerships we have with all the people around us. We must shed prejudice (verse 11) and put on humility. We must be kind and gentle but also patient and forgiving. We must seek unity and peace. We haven't even begun to address the commands given towards specific relationships (verses 18-25).

As we seek to love people according to the pattern in which Christ commands and models, we will be ever more aware of the blessings of the partnerships in our lives. Instead of complaining when our spouse doesn't take out the trash, we can be thankful that he mowed the lawn or changed the oil in the car or for the big hugs he gives. When our boss is demanding, we can appreciate that we are able to bring a home a paycheck. When someone cuts us off on the interstate, we can praise God that we didn't get hit and say a prayer that the other driver gets home safely.

When we implement a Heavenly perspective, when we apply Godly practices, and when we aim to be Christ-like in our partnerships, we will find that being "always" thankful may not be easy, but it's definitely easier. Having a thankful heart may not come naturally, but it isn't as impossible as it might first seem. If we truly want to be representatives of Jesus, then it really isn't optional. Simply put, to live like Christ is to grow in gratitude.

Notes:

March Week Four

Grow in Wisdom

Read: Colossians 4

Primary Point: We're not just commanded to go; we're also commanded to grow.

Memory Verse: "Live wisely among those who are not believers, and make the most of every opportunity." *Colossians 4:5*

Grow in Wisdom

Billy Graham once said, "Each life is made up of mistakes and learning, waiting and growing, practicing patience and being persistent."1 The author of Colossians has taught us several ways to grow in our walk with the Lord.

As the apostle Paul ties up this short book, he ends with a few personal notes and one more area in which we should cultivate our Christian life. Verse 5 tells us that we should "live wisely." Now, the Bible (especially the book of Proverbs) is full of words on wisdom, but for the purpose of this lesson, we will concentrate on two specific areas where we can grow in wisdom.

Capitalize On Opportunities

Gary Cooper had the opportunity to take the lead role in *Gone with the Wind* and refused.

In 1962, Decca Recording Company rejected the Beetles.

Atari and Hewlett-Packard weren't interested in Steve Job's and Steve Wozniak's personal computer.

Missed opportunities are hard to stomach. So, we are reminded in verse 5 that living wisely means "making the most of every opportunity."

What kinds of opportunities do you think Paul is actually referring to? Opportunities for making more money? Opportunities for self-promotion? Opportunities to live the good life? I don't think so. If we look back to verse 3 you will read his request. Paul is telling us not to miss opportunities to share the Good News of Christ. Galatians 6:10 and 2 Timothy 4:2 offer similar encouragements.

The directive is clear. Part of growing in wisdom is being attentive to and taking advantage of the opportunities we are given to influence people for the sake of the gospel.

Create Meaningful Conversations

Part of utilizing the opportunities that God gives us also involves creating meaningful conversations. Paul says that our conversations should be "gracious and attractive." Ephesians 4:29 directs that our words should be "good and helpful...an encouragement to those who hear them." Matthew 12:34 reminds us that what we say is actually a direct revelation of what is in our hearts.

Once, when the boys were little, I got behind a very slow driver. I was in a hurry to get somewhere fast and grew impatient. As I gripped the steering wheel tightly, I said, "Come on Grandpa! Move!" About that time, I saw a little head trying to peek around the seat beside me. Sjon-Paul said, "Hey, is Pa up there?"

I realized quickly that my careless words were being heard even when I thought I was talking to myself. Our words—our conversations—matter.

They have the potential to point people to Christ or drive people from Him. Our conversations have the ability to call people to hope and encouragement or contribute to their despair. As such, our responses should be more than just reactionary. In fact, if we are to grow in wisdom, we will be intentional about what comes out of our mouths.

Grow in prayer. Grow in truth. Grow in gratitude. Grow in wisdom. Colossians is a book of growth. Someone once said, "If you aren't growing, then you're dying." As Christians, that's an important lesson to remember. So, as we enjoy the blossoms on the trees and the daffodils blooming along the side of the road, let them serve as a reminder to us. We're not just commanded to go; we're also commanded to grow.

Notes:

April

Quiet Characters in the Resurrection Story

April Week One

What We Can Learn from Malchus with the Missing Ear

Read: Luke 22:50-51

Primary Point: Regardless of our circumstances, Jesus always cares.

Memory Verse: "Give all your worries and cares to God, for he cares about you." *1 Peter 5:7*

What We Can Learn from Malchus with the Missing Ear

The Last Supper. The prayer in the garden. The mock trial. The crucifixion. The resurrection. Easter. It's the story of our faith. Most of us have heard it all our lives, and as such, we may be jaded to it. We know about the betrayal of Judas. We remember the brutality of the cross. We relate to Peter's brush-off. While we celebrate the gift of salvation, the Good News has become "old hat."

If we look closely, there in the shadows of the story, are quiet characters, people whose words are not recorded, people whose names are not always mentioned, people who might otherwise be considered nobodies in the course of history. They are in God's Word for a reason. This month, let's discover four quiet characters in the resurrection story and what we can learn from them. First, let's consider Malchus.

Sometimes We Are Caught In Circumstances Beyond Our Control.

Malchus was the high priest's slave. John, the 'other disciple' who (in verse 15) is reported as being familiar with Caiaphas, the high priest, is the only gospel writer to call Malchus by name. We can assume then that John at least recognized him and may have even known him.

While we don't know exactly what being the slave of a priest entailed, it's pretty easy to believe that Malchus didn't have a choice about where he was that night. In fact, he was probably sent to be the eyes and ears of Caiaphas as the Roman soldiers and temple guards marched into the garden to arrest Jesus. While the rest of the contingency was armed with swords and knives, Malchus may have simply held a lantern to light the way. He was, after all, a slave not a soldier. He was most likely just doing his job. Even if he knew Jesus, even if he had a personal opinion, it's also unlikely that he had a choice.

Sometimes, life is like that. Like Malchus, we find ourselves in situations that stink, situations that are dangerous, situations that are out of our control. Without warning, something really bad happens; our worst fears are realized. Someone or something reaches out, swings a sword, and cuts us deeply. Sometimes, even when we didn't do anything to ask for it, we are hurt.

Sometimes It Seems As If No One Cares.

Malchus didn't defend himself, and neither did anyone else. Peter rashly swung a sword and cut off the slave's ear—cut it off! There it was—on the ground—and there was Malchus, probably on his knees with his hand pressed over the open wound, trying to staunch the blood. Perhaps he was screaming. Maybe he was crying. Maybe he just sat there in shock and silence. Nowhere do we read of anyone helping. All those men with swords, but it seemed that no one stepped in to defend Malchus. No one even offered him a band-aid.

Like Malchus, we may feel disposable. We may believe that everyone is out to get us. We may seem invisible to the world around us. When life gets tough, when people get mean, when we are alone, it's easy to believe that no one cares. Malchus probably felt that way; he was wrong.

Always, Jesus Is Our Comfort.

Malchus was bleeding and whimpering from pain, probably growing faint from the loss of blood. There was Jesus, facing the ultimate separation from His Father, just moments away from the desertion of his closest friends, and hours away from the excruciating pain of the cross. Jesus knew the heartache that lay ahead. No one would have thought any less of Him if He had, like everyone else, ignored a wounded slave who was part of that violent crowd of enemies, but Jesus cared. It was Jesus who told Peter to put his sword away, and, as Luke the physician records, it was Jesus who, with a simple touch, healed the missing ear of Malchus.

When we can't feel it, when it's hard to believe it, just remember John 3:16. God loved us enough to send Jesus, and Jesus loved us enough to willingly come, to die for us, to pay the price for our sins. People can hurt us, but no one can destroy us when our faith is in Jesus. He is our greatest source of comfort. Sometimes it may feel that Jesus is the only One who cares, but always He is enough.

Notes:

April Week Two

What We Can Learn from the Boy in the Buff

Read: Mark 14:43-52

Primary Point: What we leave can teach us a valuable lesson.

Memory Verse: "Then, calling the crowd to join his disciples, he said, 'If any of you wants to be my follower, you must give up your own way, take up your cross, and follow me.'" *Mark 8:34*

What We Can Learn from the Boy in the Buff

It is a minor story. Only one of the gospel writers even mentions it. There it is, tucked away in the book of Mark. It's so absurd that it's almost comical.

Jesus was being taken away by the Roman guards. His disciples deserted Him. The tension was thick, and nerves were frayed. There, right in the middle of Jesus's arrest story, we find a young spy.

A boy, maybe a teen, had slipped furtively behind the shrubbery and vegetation, watching the disciples sleep, listening as Jesus prayed. Can you imagine his intrigue as Jesus confronted the crowd of armed warriors? Can you imagine his shock as Peter drew his sword? Can you imagine his wonder when Jesus picked up the servant's disembodied ear and re-attached it? Can you imagine his fear and fascination as the Roman soldiers grabbed Jesus and began to lead Him away?

He must have been mesmerized, and he waited too long to get away. Then, he was discovered. Hands reached for and grabbed him. Of course, he was young and agile and with a quick turn or two, he managed to escape. Unfortunately, he left his nightclothes behind. I can almost hear the roar of the laughter as the crowd watched the boy in the buff run away.

Some theologians believe that the boy was none other than John Mark himself since the story was only told in the book carrying his name. All the other disciples had fled. He alone (among the disciples) would have known about it. Of course, even if they did, they probably wouldn't have considered the embarrassing tale worth including in the account of Christ's death and resurrection. Regardless of the reason, Mark thought it a worthy addition to God's Word. As such, it offers a few lessons for us to learn.

Fleeing Isn't Always A Bad Thing.

In all the great stories, the good guys stand up against the bad. Dorothy confronts the Wicked Witch of the West. David beats Goliath. Peter Pan fights off Captain Hook. Sometimes, in real life, though, it's better to flee—even for Christians.

It sounds almost sacrilege, but it's not. In Genesis 19, the angels took Lot and his family out of Sodom and Gomorrah, and they said, "Flee for your lives! Don't look back, and don't stop…" (Gen 19:17). In the book of Numbers, God commanded His people to establish cities where people could flee for refuge. In Psalms, David fled to God for protection. In Matthew, we read about Mary and Joseph fleeing to Egypt to escape King Herod. Later in Matthew, Jesus even commanded his disciples to flee from one city to another when persecuted (Matthew 10:23).

Sometimes, fleeing is actually the wisest course of action. For example, 1 Corinthians 6:18 tells us to flee from sexual immorality, and 2 Timothy 2:22 tells us to flee youthful passions.

That night in the garden, the boy in the buff wasn't equipped to fight a Roman army. He was wise enough to know when to flee. We can learn a lesson from him. When evil comes knocking at our door, we should remember Amos 5:14, "Do what is good, and run from evil so that you may live."

Following Christ Isn't Necessarily Safe Or Easy.

When the boy decided to follow Jesus that night, I am sure he never thought he would run into such danger. He slid out of the bed full of curiosity. I imagine he jumped back under those covers with shivers from more than the cold night air. He learned a valuable lesson. Following Christ isn't always safe or easy.

There's a reason Jesus said, "If any of you wants to be my follower, you must give up your own way, take up your cross, and follow me" (Mark 8:34). There's a reason why He spoke about the world hating believers.

As American Christians, we are immune to much of the persecution faced by Christ-followers all over the world. Even still, it is wise to remember what the boy in the buff found out the hard way. We have a lot of guarantees regarding our faith and our eternity in Heaven, but Jesus never promised us that everything in this life would be safe or easy.

Forsaking Something Is Sometimes Required.

Perhaps the most important thing we can learn from this young man's misadventure is that sometimes we have to leave something behind. Had he held too tightly to his nightshirt; the young boy may have lost his life that night.

There is an adage about how to trap a monkey. It is said that if you put a yummy treat in a bottle, the monkey will reach in to get it. Because his hand is balled up in a fist grasping his goody, he can't get his hand out of the bottle. In order to get out of the trap, he has to leave the treat behind. As the story goes, the monkey would rather stay trapped.

I wonder how much we are like that monkey? What do we refuse to give up for the kingdom of God? Mark 10:29 talks about losing a house or even family for the sake of Christ. In multiple places in scripture, believers are admonished to willingly give up money or material possessions. If there is any thing which we refuse to forsake for the cause of Christ, then that thing is actually a god in our lives. If Jesus asks, we have to be willing to leave things behind. Because, as Matthew 16:26 asks, "What do you benefit if you gain the whole world but lose your own soul?"

Think about it. Perhaps this encounter was the beginning of Mark's life of discipleship. Instead of scaring him away from the pursuit of Jesus, perhaps it was the catalyst that drove him to a lifetime of following Christ. What could have just been an embarrassing teenage tale instead provides us with valuable lessons about discipleship.

Notes:

April Week Three

What We Can Learn from Bad Guy Barabbas

Read: Mark 15:1-15

Primary Point: A gift is only good if you accept it.

Memory Verse: "For this is how God loved the world: He gave his one and only Son, so that everyone who believes in him will not perish but have eternal life." *John 3:16*

What we can learn from Bad Guy Barabbas

Perhaps one of the most notable bad guys who never even spoke a word is Barabbas. Rome traditionally gave their conquests a lot of freedom in continuing to live and worship as they pleased. However, they required a high price for those quasi freedoms. For one, the people were heavily taxed. So, revolts, like the one led by Barabbas, were not necessarily uncommon. Still, the powerful Romans usually put down insurrections easily.

Because of this interesting dynamic, the religious authorities and common people often had complicated relationships with insurrectionists. In one sense, they were heroes—or would be if they succeeded. Their efforts had the potential to provide the Jews freedom and the ability to independently govern themselves as a distinct nation. On the other hand, every time someone attempted a revolt and didn't succeed, the Roman oppression grew worse. This type of fear was actually one of the reasons that the religious authorities hated Jesus.

Perhaps Barabbas and Jesus had something in common in that regard. Maybe Barabbas had, like Jesus, been more popular before he had been caught. Perhaps just a few days before, the people had also cheered him on from the sidelines, secretly hoping that he would succeed.

It didn't matter. He had not succeeded. In fact, he, like so many others before him and so many more that would come after, had been caught. Now, he was being tried as a murderer. It didn't really matter who he had killed. It may have been a Roman centurion or government authority, someone that the average Jewish citizen would have despised. Publicly, when the insurrection had been squashed, the people would not have shown any sympathy or support for Barabbas, even if there had once been some. Doing so would have put them on "his side," a side of defiance against Rome, a side that was unsafe, that would call attention to them and their families, that would put them on the "radar" as the next possible threat.

Yet, that day, in the courtyard, standing before Pilot, they chanted for his release. They demanded his freedom in place of Jesus, who knew no sin. In the wake of his unexpected pardon, Barabbas taught us a few things.

Sometimes, We Are The Problem.

It's easy to blame others. It's easy to blame circumstances. It's easy to point the finger anywhere except at ourselves. Sometimes, though, like Barabbas, we are to blame. Sometimes the messes of our lives are simply the consequences of bad choices. We made the mistake. We did what we are accused of doing. It is our fault. In fact, the Bible tells us that in terms of sin, we are always guilty. "As the scriptures say, 'No one is righteous—not even one'" (Romans 3:10).

Sometimes, We Are Pawns.

Of course, there are also times in life when we will be used. The crowd wasn't really interested in the welfare of Barabbas. The scribes and pharisees weren't trying to convert him into a model citizen. They shouted his name not so much to save his life as to take another. Life is like that some times. We can be the hero one minute and the heel the next. People won't always treat us right. The favor of men is fickle, but the love of the Lord lasts a lifetime and beyond. 1 Chronicles 16:34 tells us, "Give thanks to the Lord, for he is good! His faithful love endures forever."

Sometimes, We Are Pardoned.

Can you imagine how ridiculous Barabbas would have looked if he said, "No, thanks. I don't want your pity. I'll just go straight to the cross. Thank you." We have no record that anything like that occurred. We have to believe that when Pilate said, "Go," Barabbas went, happily relieved if slightly confused.

While there is some speculation, no one really seems to know what happened to Barabbas after he was released. It's hard to imagine that this event did not significantly impact his life in some way. While history may have forgotten him, we should remember and learn from him, and in one way even imitate him. Through the death and resurrection of Christ, God has also offered us a pardon. Jesus paid the price for our sins. Be like Barabbas. Accept the gift.

Notes:

April Week Four

What We Can Learn from Sight-Seeing Simon

Read: Mark 15:21-25 and Luke 23:24-26

Primary Point: When God calls you down a difficult path, follow Him, and finish well.

Memory Verse: "So let's not get tired of doing what is good. At just the right time we will reap a harvest of blessing if we don't give up." *Galatians 6:9*

What we can learn from Sight-Seeing Simon

Simon of Cyrene was the man who helped carry the cross of Jesus. John doesn't mention Simon in his gospel. In fact, he says that Jesus carried the cross by Himself. So, we have to assume that Jesus started the trek to Golgotha carrying the cross by Himself. At some point, that changed. Simon was given the opportunity of a lifetime.

The gospel accounts indicate that Simon and his sons just "happened" into town. Maybe Simon was a Jew who had come from his home in North Africa to participate in the Passover celebration. Maybe he was a tradesman getting a taste of the cultural experience. We can assume that Simon got more than he bargained for when he headed into Jerusalem that day.

Can you imagine Simon and his sons standing in the crowd? Maybe they were looking for a place to grab a bite to eat when the traffic held them up. Squashed between the piles of humanity, they would have strained to see what the commotion was all about.

Maybe Simon was a strong-looking chap who was able to elbow his way to the front. If his sons were young, he might have had one hand holding tight to each son as he struggled forward against the crowd trying to get to the temple to make a sacrifice or to the home of a waiting relative.

Once on the outer edge, he couldn't have missed the bloodied and beaten men. There were three of them, struggling under the weight of the huge wooden beams across the shredded muscles and exposed bones of their backs.

Perhaps Simon was so astonished, so taken aback, that he didn't notice the Roman soldier heading his way. Then, it was too late, too late to slip quietly back into the crowd.

It was futile to resist. So, Simon—an outsider, a visitor, a tourist—was given an unusual welcoming party. He was forced to carry the cross of a condemned man—the cross of Jesus.

What seemed, at the very least, a burdensome inconvenience turned into an experience Simon would never forget. What can we learn from how he handled the situation?

Fighting Is Futile.

Sometime, God calls us to difficult tasks. Sometimes, the path that He takes us on is not a path we would have chosen for ourselves. Sometimes, it is a long and arduous road. As Christians, we should understand that fighting is futile. It will only make things more difficult.

In Luke 9:23 Jesus told us that if we want to be His followers, we should expect to carry our own kinds of crosses. We have to give up our own ways and follow Him.

Of course, God is a gentleman. Unlike the Romans, He won't impose His will on anyone. If we are seeking His blessing, His peace, and His promises, then we need to be ready to follow His will. There is no guarantee that it will be easy, but we know He'll be right by our side.

Follow The Savior's Lead.

Given that Simon was probably not a citizen of Jerusalem, he may not have known where he was supposed to go. However, Jesus knew, and Jesus led the way (Luke 23:26). Sometimes, we have no idea where we are going either. Life seems to be a complicated maze. We are just trying to navigate it the best we know how. Jesus knows where we are going, even if we don't. In John 12:26 (a) Jesus reminds us that serving God means following Him. We need to keep our eyes on Jesus. He will lead the way.

Finish Well.

Simon carried the cross all the way to the hill where Jesus was crucified. He finished the job. While we don't know what happened to him after that day, there are theories. Matthew, Mark and Luke all mention him by name; Mark even records his sons' names. Perhaps they knew him. It is possible that they knew him before the crucifixion. It is probable that they met him after.

I like to think that Simon finished well indeed. I like to imagine that he not only carried the cross of Jesus on his back, he also carried it in his heart for the rest of his life.

Galatians 6:9 tells us to "not become weary in doing good, for at the proper time we will reap a harvest if we do not give up." Whatever task Jesus calls us to do, let's be like Simon. Finish well.

Notes:

May

How to Expand Your Prayer Life

May Week One

Being Thankful in Prayer

Read: Philippians 4:6-7

Primary Point: Thanksgiving is an important part of prayer.

Memory Verse: "Devote yourselves to prayer with an alert mind and a thankful heart." *Colossians 4:2*

Being Thankful in Prayer

One day, as a young mother, I noticed the bumper sticker on a car in front of me. I can't remember what it said, but I know that it was revolting. I wondered why anyone would want something that disgusting as his identification to the world. So, I prayed out loud for the man driving the car, that someone would come into his life and introduce him to Christ, that He would have a change of heart and life.

When Sjon-Paul, who was only two or three at the time, asked what I was doing, I told him. He didn't say much, but before we could turn the corner, he pointed to another car now in front of us and said, "Mom let's pray for them." So, we did. When they pulled away, we prayed for the people in the next car. Before we reached our destination, Sjon-Paul saw a man walking down the road and said, "Mom let's pray for him." Growing a little tired of the exchanges, I said, "OK, Sjon-Paul. Why don't you pray for him?"

He said, "Thank you God for that man." I almost cried.

I thought about that man walking to work or school. I wondered if he had anyone else praying for him. I wondered what was going on in his life on that beautiful, sunny day. He had no idea that a two-year-old boy thanked God for him, but I have no doubt that God heard that simple prayer. Perhaps, just perhaps, it made a difference in that man's life.

Make no mistake. Prayer is as much about the mind as it is the heart. Yet, so many times, we put so little thought into our prayers. In fact, instead of a conversation with the Lord, we often treat prayer like a fast-food order at our favorite drive-through restaurant.

I think we pray like this because we honestly don't know a better way. Many of us are afraid that we don't have the right words, that we don't have the right methods, that we aren't doing it "right." Prayer is meant to be more than a laundry-list of requests. It's meant to be an intimate time of discussion with our Father. So, the next few lessons are devoted to learning creative and Biblical ways to improve our prayer life.

Today we begin with thanksgiving. If a small child could so easily thank God for a man he didn't even know, why can't we find things for which to be thankful as well. Here are a few useful methods to get you started.

- Before you get out of bed every morning, thank God for five things.
- When you are driving to work, come up with one thing that begins with each letter of the word "THANKS," and thank God for them.
- At the dinner table, instead of having one person pray, ask each person to contribute to the prayer by saying, "Thank you, God, for _____."
- On the way home from a child's game or activity, ask everyone to take turns thanking God for something you see out the windows.
- At bedtime, make it a habit to thank God for your spouse, family, or friends. Thank God for them individually and specifically. "Thank you, God, for Sue, for her cheerful smile and the way she makes our office a pleasant place to work."

Through the voice of my small child, God reminded me that I can never pray too much or for the wrong person, and even the smallest prayers of thanksgiving are important. I often wonder what happened to that man. I hope to find out one day in Heaven.

Notes:

May Week Two

Interceding in Prayer

Read: Ephesians 6:18, 1 Timothy 2:1-2, and Matthew 5:44

Primary Point: Pray for believers, bosses, and bullies; pray on behalf of others.

Memory Verse: "Pray in the Spirit at all times and on every occasion. Stay alert and be persistent in your prayers for all believers everywhere." *Ephesians 6:18*

Interceding in Prayer

When my sister, Marsha, was young, she was particularly mischievous. She scaled the kitchen cupboards. She escaped from the house and ran into the road. She loved to crawl in and over the pews at church. As a firm believer in corporal discipline, my Dad would inevitably pick little Marsha up and take her out of the sanctuary in order to help her "understand" the importance of sitting still and listening to the pastor.

Marsha did not go quietly.

While our pew was second from the front and therefore prime real estate for a quick exit, Marsha would whoop and holler and cry and kick, loudly and sufficiently enough to totally disrupt the service and embarrass her very well-behaved older sister.

I will never forget the pastor stopping the service and waiting for the noise to die down. Sometimes he would even say, "Let's all bow our heads and pray for Marsha!"

That's intercessory prayer. It is taking a request to the Lord on behalf of someone else. Most of us have no problem doing this for our family. We even ask God to bless our friends. We are quick to pray for people we know who are suffering from cancer or who have suffered the loss of a loved one. We might even pray for strangers who have suffered a devastating tragedy. However, we are specifically looking at creative and Biblical ways to pray this month. So, let's look at three groups that we may be leaving out of our prayers, three groups for whom scripture says we should pray.

Pray For Other Believers

In Ephesians 6, Paul, is writing to the church at Ephesus, but he isn't asking them to just pray for each other. He's commanding them to pray for all believers. Why?

Well, for one thing, believers in Paul's time were being persecuted. Guess what? Millions of Christians are being persecuted throughout the world right now. Our fellow brothers and sisters all over the world need prayers for God's protection.

That's not all. In verse 19 of this same chapter, Paul asks that the Ephesians pray for him, that he would have the words "to fearlessly make known the mystery of the gospel." In another passage, in Acts 4, we read about a group of Christians who were facing possible persecution. They didn't pray for safety. They prayed, "Enable your servants to speak your word with great boldness" (Acts 4:29).

If you want to liven up your prayer life, try this. Pray for yourself and for other believers (those you know and those you don't) to be attentive to opportunities to spread the gospel and courageous in sharing their testimonies. Pray that we would all have hearts to follow God's will and lead others to Christ. Then, watch out, because God will answer those prayers.

Pray For Our Bosses

We don't have kings here in America, but we do have a president. We also have congressmen and women, senators, governors, and mayors. We have judges and policemen and school teachers and parents and employers. In short, we have a lot of people who are in authority over us in a variety of ways.

Years ago, a parent whose young child got into trouble almost every day in school said, "I guess I shouldn't be surprised. His father and I have a problem with authority too." Authority is a sticky topic.

Romans 13:1 says, "Let everyone be subject to the governing authorities, for there is no authority except that which God has established. The authorities that exist have been established by God."

I'm not going to get into a theological or political debate on this. Let's all just agree that this verse is NOT saying that God condones people who abuse their positions of authority to hurt others, unduly promote themselves, or do any other matter of evil things. That's not what this is about. This verse is encouraging us to recognize that God is the One who established positions of authority, the first and foremost being His own.

While we cannot control who our "bosses" are in this world, the Bible tells us that we can and should pray for them. People in authority will play a role in the kind of lives we have. So, pray for them. Whether you like them or not, pray for them. Pray that they would have wisdom, that they seek God's guidance, and follow His commands. If for no other reason, pray so that perhaps we might have more quiet and peaceful lives.

Pray For The Bullies

I will never forget the night of 9/11. Our church opened its doors for a special prayer meeting. We, along with the rest of the nation, were stunned by the events at the Twin Towers. As we sat together in silence, the pastor opened the floor to prayers. One by one, people in the congregation took turns praying for the victims, for their families, for the firefighters, and emergency personnel.

Finally, one man prayed for our enemies, for the people who had orchestrated the attack, for the ones who were even at that moment somewhere celebrating the devastating loss of life.

In the dark of that sanctuary, I was both stunned and convicted.

God calls us to pray for our enemies. (He calls us to love them as well, but that's another discussion.)

Of course, many of us would say that we don't really have enemies. Maybe we don't, at least not in the traditional sense of the word. It's not like we are getting called out to a duel on the front lawn or anything. But what about…

- the person at work who talks about you behind your bac?
- the ex- who posts snide remarks about you on social media?
- the child who seems to hate you?
- the driver who rides your bumper on the freeway and then gives you the finger when passing?
- the person who vehemently opposes everything you believe in, everything you stand for, everything that makes you who you are?

We may not call them our enemies. We may not even call them "bullies," but we all have them in our lives. The Bible says pray for them.

Even though it sounds counterintuitive to everything we know about self-preservation, the Bible commands it. So, pray for the bullies in your life. Pray that God would bless them. Pray that God would give them patience. Pray that God would soften their hearts. Pray that they would have a good day. Just do it. Pray for your enemies.

Notes:

May Week Three

Praising in Prayer

Read: 1 Chronicles 16:7-36

Primary Point: Praise is a powerful and important part of prayer.

Memory Verse: "Great is the Lord! He is most worthy of praise! He is to be feared above all gods." *1 Chronicles 16:25*

Praising in Prayer

Have you ever had a moment when you felt compelled to praise the Lord? I am not talking about feeling forced to sing along in church on Sunday morning. I am talking about feeling so overwhelmed by His love, His beauty, His power, His mercy, or just His presence that you could not contain it, that you absolutely had to praise Him.

I felt that way when I stood in front of the ocean and at the foot of the Smokies, when I laid on a sun-kissed rock in the middle of a rushing mountain stream, and when I looked across the fields of wheat or grass near my home. I also felt the unmistakable urge to praise God when I held my newborn sons, when I watched them give their hearts to the Lord, when they emerged from baptism, when they celebrated great victories in their lives, and, surprisingly enough, in the middle of my anguish at my son's funeral.

Praise is showing approval or admiration for someone or something. As such, it should be a natural offspring of a Christian's life. Yet, how often do we omit this vital component from our prayers?

Perhaps, we have grown so accustomed to having someone lead us in praise and worship that we have forgotten that we have the capacity to do it on our own. Let's take a few notes from David's Song of Praise in 1 Chronicles 16 and learn some practical ways we can add praise to our prayers.

Sing To Him.

Verse 9 encourages us to sing when praising the Lord. Don't worry if you don't have a musical voice. Your praises are beautiful to the Lord, even if you can't carry a tune in a bucket. Think of hymns you learned as a child. Turn on a local Christian radio station and sing along. Look up the words to a favorite song you sing in church, and read the lyrics out loud. Songs can be a powerful way to praise.

Lift Up His Name.

In verse 10, we are encouraged to think about the names of our Lord. He has many! Start with those you know. It can be as simple as saying, "Praise you, God. I worship you, Lord. You are great, Jesus."

If you really want to get creative, try thinking of some of the Old Testament names—I AM, Jehovah, Adonai, etc. Do a little research and see how many you can find. Dig a little deeper and find out what they mean. Write your discoveries on index cards and stash them in your Bible or tape them to your mirror or the dashboard of your car. By learning and using the various names of God in our prayers, we can worship Him for Who He is, not just for the things He has done.

Remember What He's Done.

Throughout this passage and specifically in verse 12, we are encouraged to think about all the great things God has done. You can start by praising Him for the miracles He performed in the Bible. Think about them. Challenge yourself to name a certain number. "Praise you God for parting the Red Sea. You are a mighty God who healed the lepers and brought the dead back to life."

Also, remember to bring it closer to home and offer adoration for the many things He has specifically done for you. "Lord, I honor you for giving me life. I am in awe of You for how you healed my dad from cancer. I give you reverence for the ways in which you always provide for my needs."

Think About Salvation.

We see this admonition in verse 15. While this passage specifically speaks of God's covenant with Israel to bring them into the Promised Land, it is also an encouragement for us to remember our salvation as the covenant we have with God through His son, Jesus. Our hearts should be full of adoration for the Father who didn't leave us to die in our sins, for the Son who gave His life to save us from our sins, and for the Holy Spirit who lives within us, gives us hope, and helps us to conquer our sins. We shouldn't take it for granted. Let's give God glory for the most precious gift of our salvation.

Rejoice With Creation.

In the verses before and after verse 30, we read a lot about nature: the world, the heavens, the earth, the sea, the fields, the crops, the trees, the forest. Let's consider how we can use nature as an inspiration to rejoice in the Lord. We can look at the beauty around us and express awe to the Creator. We can think about the intricate and delicate designs and praise God for His artistry. We can begin with A and see how far we can work towards Z, praising God about various plants or animals or other aspects of nature. It's OK to be creative when we honor God.

In Luke 19:40, as Jesus traveled down the Mount of Olives, some of the followers of Jesus began to sing and praise Him as they walked along. When the Pharisees rebuked them, Jesus said, "If they kept quiet, the stones along the road would burst into cheers!"

Do we really want it to be said of us that the rocks had to do the job for which we were created? Praise should come easily to our lips for a God who has been so generous to us. Let's not forget to worship and praise our Lord in prayer.

Notes:

May Week Four

Why Confession Counts

Read: 1 John 1:8-10

Primary Point: Confession helps keep our souls clean.

Memory Verse: "But if we confess our sins to him, he is faithful and just to forgive us our sins and to cleanse us from all wickedness." *1 John 1:9*

Why Confession Counts

Boys fight. Boys fight a lot. Surprisingly (note the sarcasm here), whenever I confronted my sons about a fight, it was always someone else's fault. It seems that, like Adam and Eve, they always wanted to point the finger at each other. I don't remember a single time one of them said, "Yep, Mom, it was my fault. I started it. I did it. I'm sorry."

It's human nature. We are often unwilling to confess our mistakes, our shortcomings, our sins—not only to one another but more importantly to God. We know that He knows. Still, by skirting around the issue, we forfeit many blessings. Since confession and repentance are essential to a productive prayer life, let's take a deeper look at this area of prayer and why it is so important.

Confession is an admission of guilt. Without confession, you can't make it to repentance, which involves remorse and a willingness to turn away from the wrongful action. If one of my boys had confessed, he might have said something like, "I hit my brother first." If he confessed and repented, he would have said something like, "Mommy, I hit my brother, and I'm sorry that I did. I will try not to do that again." If his heart was right, then his statement would have been sincere and not just something he uttered to get out of a punishment.

In Romans 3:23, we are told that everyone sins. In Romans 6:23, we are told that the result of our sins is death.

1 John 1:9 tells us, "If we confess our sins, He is faithful and just to forgive us our sins and to cleanse us from all unrighteousness."

Therefore, confession and repentance are essential to the salvation message. In that moment, when we give ourselves fully to the Lord, Christ forgives our sins—past, present, and future. However, that doesn't mean that confession and repentance should then be forgotten.

I don't think it is a surprise to any of you, but just in case, I will let you in on a little secret. Even after we get saved, we are still sinners. We still mess up; we still make mistakes; we still sin. As a result, we still need to confess our sins to the Lord, ask for forgiveness, and turn towards a better way.

Our sins are like dirty clothes. When we confess our sins to God and ask for His forgiveness, God gives us a spiritual bath and puts new clothes on us. Just as importantly, since we are now His children, He promises that He will continue to do that until we get to Heaven. However, too often, we "get dirty" and come home to the Lord and pretend that we are not. When we come to the Lord in prayer without confession and repentance, it's like we are sitting down at the table with Him and pretending He can't see that big old stain right in the middle of our chest. When we ask for His blessings on our lives without confession and repentance, it's as if we are putting new clothes on top of our dirty rags.

Verses throughout the Bible tell us about the dangers of concealing our sins. 1 John 1: 8-10 goes so far as to say, "If we claim we have no sin, we are only fooling ourselves and not living in the truth. If we confess our sins to him, he is faithful and just to forgive us our sins and to cleanse us from all wickedness. If we claim we have not sinned, we are calling God a liar and showing that his word has no place in our hearts."

The longer we are Christians, the more our outward actions should be like Christ. In other words, we aren't likely to be the town drunks, murderers, or thieves. However, just because we don't "look" sinful doesn't mean that we are saints. We are all sinners. The closer we grow to the Lord, the more we should recognize the sinful nature of our hearts and minds as well as our bodies. Here are a few suggestions on how we can make sure that we come CLEAN in our prayers.

Confess sins early in the prayer. Think of it like the dinner analogy we discussed before. We want to come before the Lord clean, but we can't do it on our own. Only He has the power to wash our sins away.

Listen to the conviction of the Spirit exposing areas that need to be brought before God. Start with the mind. Pray for any areas of sin regarding thoughts. Move to the heart. Confess areas where emotions or attitudes have been sinful. End by confessing any sinful actions.

Eagerly repent of sins. Remember this requires not only naming sins but expressing sincere sorrow over them.

Accept God's forgiveness. God promises that if we repent of our sins, He will forgive them. Accept those beautiful gifts of grace and mercy with thanksgiving.

Note the sins that have been confessed and repented of and try to recognize them in the future. Learn from mistakes and avoid making them again. Consider the circumstances that surround repetitive sins and consider drastic actions that may need to be taken to get out of that cycle.

Remember, just like we take baths daily to keep our bodies clean, we need to spend time in confession and repentance with the Lord to keep our souls clean. We don't neglect our bodily hygiene; let's not neglect our spiritual hygiene either. Make confession and repentance a daily habit.

Notes:

May Week Five

Being Silent in Prayer

Read: Psalm 62:5-8

Primary Point: If you don't want your conversation to be one-sided, practice silence with God.

Memory Verse: "Let all that I am wait quietly before God, for my hope is in him." *Psalm 62:5*

Being Silent in Prayer

When my husband, Ian, was young, he was evidently quite the talker. At some point, a family friend offered him 25 cents to be quiet for 1 minute. "Back then," a quarter was a lot of money! So, as Ian says, he "zipped it." What seemed like an eternity passed. When he could take it no longer, he shouted, "How much time do I have left?" to which the friend replied, "Nope, you didn't make it."

Silence can be hard for many of us. In fact, for those of us who especially like to talk, this may be one of the hardest spiritual disciplines. While it may be neglected, it is still very necessary.

Being quiet before God allows us to better hear His voice through His Word and through the promptings of the Holy Spirit. This type of silence involves not just an external muting of noise and distractions but also an internal hushing of our own thoughts. As such, silence in prayer is something that requires intentionality. Let's consider a few things as we seek to add this dimension to our prayer times.

Rest Before

There is nothing wrong with whispering prayers to God in those sweet moments before we doze off to sleep. However, when it comes to being quiet in God's presence, sleepiness isn't likely to make silence easier. Since the point of being quiet in

God's presence is to actually listen for His voice, it is best to come well rested.

Remove Yourself

We do not live in a quiet culture. We are surrounded by so much noise that silence actually makes many people uncomfortable. How many homes have a television running even when no one is watching? How often do we get in the car and immediately turn on the radio? When we are preparing to converse with God, we should eliminate as many distractions as possible. Turn off electronic devices. If we know that a sink of dirty dishes is going to distract us, we shouldn't sit at the kitchen table with it in view. We should find a place of solitude where we won't be interrupted.

Relieve Your Mind

While I'm not talking about some New Age Zen-type of meditation, it is important to quiet our own inner voices in order to hear God. For me, this is extremely difficult. Less than 30 seconds into my quiet time, I usually find myself making mental grocery and to-do lists. In order to help alleviate those natural tendencies, you can take a few minutes before you begin your prayer time. Spend the time writing down anything that is on your mind: your lists, your worries, your plans for the day, things to do, etc. Then, you can set them aside without worrying that you may forget something important.

Redirect Your Thoughts

Spend time reading or listening to scripture before you pray. If you still have trouble shutting off your own thoughts, try setting a timer for one minute and intentionally listen until the timer goes off. You can gradually increase the time as you become more adept at the practice. You may also want to spend a few seconds whispering the name of Jesus out loud to yourself before you begin.

Resolve To Just Do It

Don't just think about including silence in your prayers. Make a plan. In this series, silence is the fifth element of prayer we have studied. While there are others, most of them could fall under one of these categories. For example, requests can be included in intercession (even if you are interceding for yourself). Think about the various elements you want to include in your prayers and arrange them in the order you want to use. I personally use something like this: Praise, Confession, Intercession (and Requests), Thanksgiving (and more Praise), and Silence.

After determining your plan, work through each area during your prayer time. While this study has been about prayer, incorporating scripture reading into your quiet time is also very important. So, you may want to read scripture, pray, listen, and then reread scripture again.

Silence is hard, but if prayer is the way in which we communicate with God, do we really want our conversations to be completely one-sided? At some point, we have to quit talking and start listening. Why not start today?

Notes:

June

Dealing with Difficult Emotions

June Week One

Why Christians Should Remain Self-Controlled

Read: Ephesians 4:26-31

Primary Point: Anger doesn't have to dictate how you act.

Memory Verse: "And 'don't sin by letting anger control you.' Don't let the sun go down while you are still angry." *Ephesians 4:26*

Why Christians Should Remain Self-Controlled

When the boys were young, I lost my temper too often. There was one particular instance that stands out in my mind. I cannot remember what Sjon-Paul was doing. I just know that we needed to be somewhere. I was in a hurry, and he wasn't cooperating. I finally had enough. I vividly remember dropping my purse and angrily rushing forward to give him what he deserved. Before I knew what happened, I was on my knees with my face flat to the floor.

My feet had gotten tangled in my purse straps. That may have been the logistical reason I fell, but I knew. God put me in that position. He stopped me in my tracks. "Not in anger, not like that," He seemed to be telling me.

Anger is a difficult emotion. It's one to which we can all relate. Sometimes our anger is justifiable, like Jesus's response to the greedy, dishonest merchants in His Father's house. However, more often than not, our anger is not righteous; it is, instead, a response that rises out of our own selfish hearts.

Let's get this straight. Emotions are not sinful. God made us human, and in our humanity, He gave us emotions. Emotions are one of the ways in which we experience God, each other, and the world around us. Anger is not sinful in and of itself, but it can definitely lead to sin. So, it's important that we learn how to handle our anger in a Godly way.

Don't Let Anger Control You

We cannot always change how we feel about a situation. However, our actions should not be a result of our emotions. Often, we react out of anger. We argue. We say and do things that we know God would not endorse. We allow our anger to control us instead of controlling our anger.

Years ago, I knew someone who would often lose her temper. She would get mad and yell and take it out on everyone around her. Her attitude and explanation were, "That's just me. That's the way I am. I can't do anything about it."

For Christians, that's simply not true. While some of us may naturally have shorter fuses, that doesn't give any of us an excuse to sin. So, how can we control our anger?

1. Pray. Counting to ten may help some people, but the better answer is to give it to God. When you feel your ire rising, take a deep breath and call on Jesus. We make jokes about it all the time, but truthfully, there is nothing more powerful than "Help me, Jesus" for the Christian warrior.

2. Step away. If at all possible, remove yourself from the situation for a while. We aren't ostriches; we can't just bury our heads in the sand and pretend that a situation doesn't exist. Still, getting away, even for a few minutes, can give us a clearer perspective. Allow yourself to calm down and seriously consider how to handle your emotions in a Christ-like manner.

3. Attack the problem, not a person. Take an academic approach to what's bothering you. Write down the problem. Brainstorm solutions. Use your anger to help resolve the problem instead of lashing out at people. You can't correct every situation, but doing this will always be a better use of your time.

Don't Let Anger Consume You

Like a seed being planted in the ground, what we carry with us to bed at night will often take root and be even harder to pull out the next day. Let's face it, though. Not every problem can be resolved before we say good-night. That's why it's important to separate what we feel from what we are facing. Just because the issue still stands does not mean that we have to hold on to the emotions surrounding it. Obviously, if we need to make amends with a person, we should do so as quickly as possible, but even more importantly, we should take our feelings to God and leave them at His feet. By giving our anger to God, we are, in essence, giving Him control. We can trust Him to handle it and sleep better without all the baggage.

Don't Condone Angry Behaviors

In verse 31, anger sits right in the middle of what is described as "evil behavior"—bitterness, rage, harsh words, and slander. Though not sinful in itself, anger can lead to sin, and it will lead to sin if it is left unchecked. Even justifiable anger does not condone sinful behavior. Thankfully, God gives us a good course of action to help curtail our natural tendencies towards wrong attitudes and actions. In verse 32, He gives us an "instead." When we are angry (yes—even when we are angry), we should "be kind to one another, tenderhearted, forgiving one another." We should treat others the same way that God treats us, with love, mercy, grace, and respect. Honestly, it's hard to stay angry when you are focusing on doing or saying something nice. *

That day so long ago, when Sjon-Paul was misbehaving, he didn't get disciplined. I was too busy recovering from my own lesson.

God disciplined me with as much surety as I had planned on disciplining my son. God certainly has a sense of humor, and it was a lesson I have not forgotten.

Jesus may not have seemed very nice when He turned over the tables in the temple (Mark 11:15-18). Discipline is rarely perceived as kindness. However, as every parent knows, while it should be given out of love and in the appropriate manner, discipline is essential. As our perfect, sinless Savior, we know that Jesus handles His righteous indignation with the proper attitude and actions and self-control. Unfortunately, we don't usually do the same. So, it's important to stay conscious of our heart and not try to excuse or justify our angry actions.

Notes:

June Week Two

What to Do When You're Afraid

Read: Psalm 56

Primary Point: Don't let fear cause you to fail; trust your Father.

Memory Verse: "But when I am afraid, I will put my trust in you." *Psalm 56:3*

What to Do When You Are Afraid

According to some sources, there are 365 admonitions in God's Word to "not fear" or "fear not." That's one for every day of the year. When something is mentioned that often, we can assume it's pretty important. Some might say that since fear is something God tells us not to do, then being afraid is sinful. To the extent that we are born sinners, and fear is a natural byproduct of the curse, I would agree. However, when I think of God's continual discussion on the matter, I tend to look at it from a different perspective.

You see, when my son Ryan was little, he was terribly afraid of storms. If the sky grew dark and thunder started to rumble, he would run and hide—often under the covers in our big bed. If I was nearby, he would jump in my lap and bury his head in my shoulder.

What did I do in those situations? Did I push him away? Did I chase him out from under the covers? Did I discipline him or admonish him because he was frightened?

Of course not. I held him tight. I loved on him, and I told him, "Ryan, you don't have to be afraid. It's just a storm. You're safe here."

I didn't want Ryan to be scared, but it had nothing to do with some arbitrary rule that I created. I didn't want him to be scared because I love him, and I know that being scared isn't a pleasant emotion. While there is such a thing as a "healthy fear," I know that often fear holds us back.

That's the way it is with God. God isn't yelling at us, "Don't be scared, you big Fraidy Cat!" He's saying, "Child, it's OK. There is no reason to be afraid. I love you. I am here." He wants us to experience life to the fullest, and we can't do that when we are afraid. In Psalm 56, David is rightfully afraid. He is in physical danger. We can learn a lot from how he responds to his fear.

He Talked To God.

Notice, David doesn't run to his military commander to express his fear. He doesn't talk to his body guards or his friends. He goes straight to the source of comfort and strength, God Himself. When he was afraid, David talked to God. He poured out his heart to God. He asked God for help.

He Trusted God.

David made a conscious decision to trust God, even when the circumstances looked grim. Trust is believing in God's ability to rectify the situation however He sees best. David knew that God could take care of him, that God would do what was best. He realized that no matter what humans could or could not do to him, God had ultimate control.

He Praised God.

Even in his fear, David recognized that God is worthy of praise and worship. So, David praised Him. David didn't know what the immediate outcome of his situation would be, but He knew who God is, and he knew that God cared for him. Because of that knowledge David could praise God even in the storms of his life.

He Remembered God's Promises.

David knew the promises of God. He didn't know all the details about how those promises would be fulfilled, but he knew what God said, and he believed it. Knowing God's Word helped David have confidence that the future was hopeful.

He Thanked God.

We tend to think of David in terms of his victories: when he killed Goliath, when the people hailed him as a hero, when he sat on the throne as king. We forget that David spent a lot of his life in battles against enemies, against former friends, and even against family. Still, David knew that he was blessed, and he spent time thanking God for those blessings.

He Walked With God.

Despite his fear, despite the dire circumstances, despite how he felt, David walked with the Lord. He was not a perfect man in any sense, but He loved God and tried to follow His ways. Even when David was afraid, he didn't turn from God.

We may not have an army at our heels, but life today can be just as scary. Like David, when we are afraid, we should talk to God, trust and praise God, remember God's promises, thank God, and walk with God. Like most of our emotions, whether fear becomes a sin is determined by what we do with it. If fear serves as a reminder not to do something dangerous or foolish (like not playing with fire), it's a good thing. If fear keeps us from doing what God has called us to do or from living the kind of life God wants us to live, it's bad. Following David's example can help us know the difference.

Notes:

June Week Three

Things to Remember When Grief's Got You Down

Read: Psalm 23

Primary Point: Grief is complex and cumbersome, but it should not be consuming.

Memory Verse: "Surely your goodness and unfailing love will pursue me all the days of my life, and I will live in the house of the Lord forever." *Psalm 23:6*

Things to Remember When Grief's Got You Down

When the boys were young, we had a three-legged dog named Pepper. Pepper had been a part of our family since before Sjon-Paul was born. As the boys grew older, so did Pepper, and eventually, he passed away. We said our good-byes and tearfully buried our pet in the yard. As we were reentering the house, I heard one of the younger boys, who had been less emotional, say to his older sibling, "Hit me! Hit me so I can cry for Pepper too."

It wasn't that my son wasn't sad. He just didn't feel or express his sadness in the same way. Grief is a very individual thing.

Sometimes we cry. Sometimes we brood. Sometimes we get angry. Sometimes we get depressed. There are cycles and stages that have been defined. There are books and pills and all manner of cheery antidotes that are often prescribed.

Grief isn't so much a difficult path to travel or a pit of quick-sand to escape; it's more like a very heavy burden. Your choice is to learn to move through life with it or to fall under the weight of it. Grief is definitely a difficult emotion. However, even in grief, God's Word gives us things to remember.

Because Of Grief, We Yearn For Heaven More.

2 Corinthians 4:18 says, "So, we don't look at the troubles we can see now; rather, we fix our gaze on things that cannot be seen. For the things we see now will soon be gone, but the things we cannot see will last forever."

This earth is not the Christian's home. While grief is never a pleasant thing, we can find solace in the fact that we have an eternal home where there will be no more pain or death, no more sorrow or tears. (Revelation 21:4)

Through Grief, We Are Able To Minister To Others Better.

In 2 Corinthians 1:4, we are reminded that God comforts us so that we can help others who experience similar trials. As long as we are a part of this world, there will be sadness and sickness and sorrow. Grief can help us to empathize with and comfort others who experience similar losses to our own. It gives us the opportunity to share the love of Christ with others who are hurting. 2 Thessalonians 2:16-17 encourages us to accept Christ's comfort so that we can have the strength to continue to do good in His name.

In Our Grief, We Are Drawn Closer To God.

Matthew 5:4 says, "God blesses those who mourn, for they will be comforted." While God is always near His followers, He seems to promise an extra measure of Himself to those who are mourning. While human comforts may fail, the Lord will be faithful. In Isaiah 66:13, God tells His people that He will comfort them like a mother. Think of a mother lovingly rocking her crying child to sleep; that is the way God wants to comfort us.

Of course, if you, like me, are still in the throes of grief, none of this really makes anything easier. Even as Christians, even when we know these things, grief is still hard. It is complex and cumbersome and, if we are not very careful, it can become consuming. That's why it's important to remember—even when we don't feel it—God is with us. God does care. Even in the messiness of grief, His love is true. Our objective then must be to hold tight to Him. We will hurt, but God still heals.

Notes:

June Week Four

A Juxtaposition of Jealousy and Why It Matters

Read: James 3:14-16

Primary Point: Why we are jealous reveals whether we're justified.

Memory Verse: "For jealousy and selfishness are not God's kind of wisdom. Such things are earthly, unspiritual, and demonic." *James 3:15*

A Juxtaposition of Jealousy and Why It Matters

Greek philosopher Antisthenes once said, "As iron is eaten away by rust, so the envious are consumed by their passion."2

Jealousy, envy, covetousness…all words for the same difficult feeling, the consuming desire for something/someone that is not our own. While we often think of jealousy in terms of romantic relationships, the emotion can surface in a variety of situations. We can find ourselves jealous of the neighbor's newly renovated house. We can be envious of our friend's promotion. We can covet the "perfect" family that sits in the pew two rows in front of us at church.

Since most of us would agree that there is nothing wrong with wanting something better, what then could really be wrong with jealousy? Let's take a closer look at this confusing emotion.

Doesn't The Bible Describe God As Jealous?

Yes, in several different locations, the Bible describes God as jealous. I don't know Greek or Hebrew. So, I'm not going to try to give you a theological breakdown of all the verses. However, I do have a degree in English (for what that's worth), and I do understand the basics of reading a dictionary. There are obviously several definitions for the word "jealous." The first definition we have already touched upon. According to Merriam Webster, another definition is "vigilant in guarding a possession." Let's look at one specific passage, Deuteronomy 4:23-24, to understand.

In the preceding verses, Moses is warning the Israelites against idolatry. He is telling them how very dangerous it is to bring about the wrath of the Lord.

Then he says, "So be careful not to break the covenant the Lord your God has made with you. Do not make idols of any shape or form, for the Lord your God has forbidden this. The Lord your God is a devouring fire; he is a jealous God."

Paraphrased, it could read, "Be careful! Don't break the covenant the Lord your God has made with you by making idols. The Lord forbids this, and He is a devouring fire; He guards His possessions."

In other words, God knows the dangers of idolatry. He knows the falsehoods associated with false worship, and He knows the separation (from Himself) that would result from His people making that choice. So, He is jealous—protective—of His people. He doesn't want to share them with anyone or anything that might bring them harm. So, yes, in this sense, God is a very jealous God.

So, Then, Is Jealousy Really A Sin?

Since we know that God is holy and cannot sin, we can be certain that His type of jealousy is not sinful. There are, in fact, times in the Bible when the word "jealousy" is used with humans in a non-sinful way. (For example, as with Paul in 2 Corinthians 11:2)

However, because we are imperfect creatures, jealousy is one of those emotions that often leads us to sin. Remember, emotions themselves are not necessarily sinful. In the case of jealousy, why we become jealous as well as what we do with our jealousy determines whether or not we have sinned.

Let's look at our key verses for more information. James 3:14-16 says, "But if you are <u>bitterly jealous</u> and there is <u>selfish ambition</u> in your heart, don't cover up the truth with boasting and lying. For <u>jealousy</u> and <u>selfishness</u> are not God's kind of wisdom. Such things are earthly, unspiritual, and demonic. For wherever there is <u>jealousy</u> and <u>selfish ambition</u>, there you will find disorder and evil of every kind."

These verses can help us in several ways. Look at the adverbs and other words which are paired with the words "jealous" and "jealousy." Words such as "bitterly" and "selfishness" give us a hint as to what has happened here. What may have begun as a slight feeling has grown into something much more. It has taken root and developed into an attitude of bitterness and resulted in selfishness. James is warning that these kinds of issues—if not dealt with immediately—can lead to even more serious actions of disorder and evil.

What's The Test?

While jealousy is sometimes used in good ways in the Bible (in reference to God and man), often it is explicitly forbidden. Galatians 5:19 lists jealousy and envy among a range of sins that result from following our evil desires, and the chapter ends with a direct command not to be "jealous of one another." Exodus 20:17 commands us not to "covet your neighbor's house. You must not covet your neighbor's wife, male or female servant, ox or donkey, or anything else that belongs to your neighbor." If you are wanting something that doesn't belong to you, chances are good that you are sinning and that you are heading down a very dangerous path.

Remember Hebrews 13:5, which says, "Don't love money; be satisfied with what you have. For God has said, 'I will never fail you. I will never abandon you.'"

God calls us to be like Him; so, if we are ever in doubt about anything we are feeling, we need to think about the character of God Himself. If we can compare the feelings that we are having with something God Himself might experience as a sense of protection, love, and diligence for the best interest of ourselves and those around us, then our sense of jealousy may actually be justified.

If not, then we need to reconsider and repent. When we feel a twinge of jealousy rising up within us, for whatever reason, our best course of action is to take it to the Lord, to pray over it, and to ask for God's help in "nipping it in the bud" before it morphs into something far worse than a difficult emotion.

Notes:

July

Lessons in Christian Freedom

July Week One

Free from Sin and Death

Read: Romans 8:1-4

Primary Point: Freedom from sin and death is something worth celebrating.

Memory Verse: "And because you belong to him, the power of the life-giving Spirit has freed you from the power of sin that leads to death." *Romans 8:2*

Free from Sin and Death

Freedom. It's something we should never take for granted. It's the time of year, perhaps more than any other, when Americans think about the freedoms we have. As we wolf down hamburgers, wave flags, and watch fireworks, we (hopefully) also think about all the sacrifices that have been made for us to enjoy these and so many other pleasantries. As Christians, it is also the perfect time to consider the freedoms we have in Christ—what we have been freed from and why we have been granted freedom.

We Are Born Slaves To Sin.

We are born sinners. This isn't just a theological point. Most parents would readily agree. You don't have to teach a child to do bad; you have to teach a child to do good. The Bible tells us in Romans 3:23 that we are all sinners. We all fall short of God's holiness. Because of this, we are essentially slaves to our own sinful human nature. Most people don't question this. We know, more than anyone else, our own imperfections, our own sinfulness. If in fact, you think you're not a sinner, ask someone who knows you well. They will probably help you figure that out.

Sin Leads To Death.

Romans 6:23 tells us that the "wages" of sin is death. In other words, sin leads to death. Looking at this from a purely physical standpoint, you may wonder how this is true. After all, not everyone dies as a result from a sinful action, right? Yes and no. While every specific death is not a result of a sinful act, death itself is a result of sin. Death was not part of God's original plan for humanity, but there were consequences for disobeying God's one rule in the Garden of Eden. After Adam and Eve disobeyed God and ate of the forbidden fruit, part of their punishment was that they had to die. From that point in time, death was as much a part of life as birth.

Christ Paid The Debt.

God is holy, and we are not. Holiness and sinfulness are like oil and water; they don't mix. However, God loves us so much that He wasn't satisfied to leave us in our sinful, dying state. Romans 5:8 tells us that God made a way to free us from this bondage. While the penalty for sin is death, God sent His son, Christ, the only sinless, perfect person to walk this earth, to die, to pay the price for us. As fully human and fully God, Jesus is perfect in every sense of the word. Therefore, He didn't just die and conquer sin, He also rose and conquered death.

Freedom Is A Gift.

That brings us back to our slavery. We are born sinners, in slavery to sin and, therefore, death. The price has been paid, and death has been conquered. Freedom is ours for the taking. Romans 10:9-10 says, "If you openly declare that Jesus is Lord and believe in your heart that God raised him from the dead, you will be saved. For it is by believing in your heart that you are made right with God, and it is by openly declaring your faith that you are saved." We accept God's free gift of salvation by confessing our sinfulness and need for a Savior and then believing and declaring our faith in Jesus as that Savior. Through salvation, we are made free.

Does that mean we won't sin anymore? Unfortunately, no. As humans, it is impossible to live perfectly, but sin should no longer be our master, and we never have to fear death again. While our mortal bodies are destined to die, we can be assured that, like our primary passage says, through the Spirit, God will give us life again—an eternal life in Heaven. Now that's freedom, and it's definitely something to celebrate.

If you want to learn more about the free gift of salvation, you can check out the complete Romans Road included at the back of this book, or contact Tricia Brown at tricia.brown@thegirlsgettogether.com.

Notes:

July Week Two

Free to Live Well with God

Read: Romans 12

Primary Point: We have been freed for a purpose—to please our Lord.

Memory Verse: "But now you are free from the power of sin and have become slaves of God. Now you do those things that lead to holiness and result in eternal life." *Romans 6:22*

Free to Live Well with God

Slavery has a deservedly bad connotation in our culture. No one likes the idea of being a slave to anyone. Especially as American citizens, we pride ourselves on our freedom. So, verses like Romans 6:22 can therefore set our teeth on edge. How can we, in one lesson, celebrate the freedom we have been given in Christ and in the next talk about being slaves to God?

I thought about writing a brief paragraph explaining the role of slavery in Biblical times. I thought about including some other scriptures and an explanation of voluntary slavery. I thought about getting historical and theological, but then, I thought again.

Basically, there is only one important thing to remember if we are offended or if we recoil when thinking about being a slave to God.

We Are Always Going To Be Slaves To Something.

Some people are, unfortunately and wrongly, slaves to other people. Some people are slaves to Satan and his demonic forces. Some people are slaves to sinful behaviors. Some people are slaves to money. Some people are simply slaves to their own ever-changing whims. Whatever controls us is our master.

We may not like it, but that's the truth. So, when Paul tells us that Christians are slaves to God, it really is a good thing because, after all, God is good. God is loving. God is merciful and gracious. God is all-knowing and therefore, knows what is best for me, for us. God is a much better and wiser master than I could ever be.

As we learned in the last lesson, when we give our lives to the Lord, He frees us from the bondages of sin and death. We are no longer in slavery to our human, sinful natures, but we are willing servants of the Most High God. Therefore, our freedom in Christ should naturally lead to a single question.

Since Christ Is Our Master, How Does He Want Us To Live?

While the Bible is full of guidance on this, for the purpose of this series, we will stick to the instructions given in Romans 12. We have been given freedom so that we can live well with God, live well with ourselves, and live well with others. Living well with God is, in essence, trying to live a life of holiness, and, therefore, encompasses the other two.

Specifically, according to Romans 12:1, living well with God means that we should give our bodies, lives and minds to God. We shouldn't do anything to ourselves or allow anything to be done to us that God would find objectionable. We should consider what He wants from our lives and take that into consideration more than what we want for ourselves. We should allow Him to change not only the way we think but also what we think about. In addition, God call us to

- Hate what is sinful. This doesn't mean hate the sinner. It means that sin—especially our own sin—should be distasteful to us. It should make us angry. It should make us sad.
- Hold onto what is good. We have the freedom in Christ to love and enjoy the good things in life that God has provided for us.

- Pray. We have the freedom in Christ to communicate with God. In addition, God loves us and desires to communicate with us.
- Be humble. In order to live rightly with Christ, as obedient servants to God, we have to remember our place. He is God. We are not.
- Do what all men know is right and good. Even in a world where relativity seems to reign, there is among most people a standard of right and wrong. For example, even the most liberal among us will usually agree that sharing is good and murder is wrong. Of course, holy living doesn't stop with a generic moral code, but it is a start.

American citizens are free, but there are still limitations to our freedoms. There are still laws that we must obey. There are still obligations to responsible citizenship. As Christians, Christ has given us freedom. He has freed us from sin and death, but we also have been freed for a purpose. We have been freed to live well with our God, to live holy lives that are pleasing to Him and good for us and for others. Let's not take our freedom for granted. Let's live as good citizens of the Kingdom of God.

Notes:

July Week Three

Free to Live Well with Ourselves

Read: Romans 12 and Psalm 139:13-16

Primary Point: Through Christ you can have poise, peace, and a purpose with the person in the mirror.

Memory Verse: "Thank you for making me so wonderfully complex! Your workmanship is marvelous—how well I know it." *Psalm 139:14*

Free to Live Well with Ourselves

Author and pastor Paul Tripp once said, "No one is more influential in your life than you are, because no one talks to you as much as you talk to yourself."3

Let that sink in for a minute.

We all have an inner voice, and whether we want to admit it or not, we all talk to ourselves. For years, scientists and doctors have studied how our self-talk affects our self-esteem, our emotional and even our physical well-being. All of their findings can be boiled into one simple nutshell. The way we talk to ourselves matters. Input directly affects output. Yet, unfortunately, we often say things to ourselves that we would never say to someone else.

That's why this aspect of Christian freedom is so important. Through our relationship with Christ, we, as Christians, have been given the freedom to live well with ourselves. You can have poise, peace, and purpose in your relationship with the person you see in the mirror.

Live With Poise

Confidence, calmness, self-assurance—do these seem contrary to your idea of a Christian personality? They are not. Yes, Christians are called to be humble, but humility means not thinking more of ourselves than we ought. It does not mean thinking less of ourselves than we should. At the beginning of Romans 12, Christians are called to be living sacrifices—presenting themselves, their lives, to the Lord for His service. I want you to consider for a moment what kind of sacrifices God required His people to bring. He didn't accept just anything, you know. He didn't want the second-hand, the runts, or the outcasts. He wanted the first fruits, the best, the unblemished. So, if God is asking us to give ourselves to Him, it demonstrates our value in His eyes. He gave His Son to die for us; we are His prized possessions.

God's Word clearly tells us that we should love our neighbors as ourselves (Matthew 22:39). This verse is making the assumption that we already love ourselves. While we should honestly evaluate ourselves, God does not take joy in watching us demean ourselves. He does not want us to flagellate ourselves physically, mentally, or spiritually. How many parents do you know who would be happy to find their children harming themselves? It would hurt us deeply to make that discovery. God the Father is the same. If we continually put ourselves down, we are in essence saying that He made a mistake, that He messed up in some way by creating us.

Through Christ, we can maintain poise and dignity in a world that struggles to value human life and worth. We can live well with ourselves by knowing how to accentuate our strengths and strengthen our weaknesses. In addition, we are blessed to be able to call on the Lord for His guidance and help.

Live In Peace

Because of our relationship with Christ, we can also live in peace with ourselves. We don't have to worry about our past mistakes; God has forgiven and forgotten our sins. We don't have to worry about the future; God promises to be with us no matter what may come.

As believers, we have the Holy Spirit convicting us of our sins and teaching us to live more Christ-like lives. If something bad happens, we can face it head-on with God's help and the hope of a better tomorrow. When we don't have the answers we need, we can ask the Lord to guide us in the way we should go. In a culture that is fearful about so many things, we can have the freedom to live in peace. We are unafraid because we know that God is in control, and our security is in Him.

Live With Purpose

Finally, we can live well with ourselves because God has given us a purpose. He compares Christians (as a group) to a body. Each of us, He says, are like a different part of the body, with a different function to serve. Together, we all work to glorify Him.

We don't have to wander aimlessly through this life wondering what we are doing, why we are here, whether or not any of it matters. We are daughters of the King, and we know that our purpose is to love and serve Him and to tell others about Him. We are also blessed to be given unique talents and abilities to carry out that purpose.

Christ has set us free from the bondage of sin and death so that we can live in freedom. Jesus bridged the gap to make a way for us, as sinful creatures, to have a relationship with a perfect, holy God. God's love for us enables us to live well with ourselves with poise, peace, and a purpose.

So, the next time we talk to ourselves, we need to remember these things. God values us very much. He wants us to live in forgiveness, without fear and anxiety. He has given us the freedom; it's up to us to live free.

Notes:

July Week Four

Free to Live Well with Others

Read: Romans 12 and Galatians 5:13-14

Primary Point: You have liberty so you can love others.

Memory Verse: "For you have been called to live in freedom, my brothers and sisters. But don't use your freedom to satisfy your sinful nature. Instead, use your freedom to serve one another in love." *Galatians 5:13*

Free to Live Well with Others

In the weeks after my son, Brandon, died, I remember having some very unusual thoughts and feelings. My brain was foggy, and my heart was broken. But life just keeps going—even after a significant loss. So, I still had to run errands. I still had to pay bills. I still went to work. I still went grocery shopping.

During that time, I would sometimes tear up unexpectedly. Sometimes I made stupid errors or asked dumb questions. Often, I just felt bad. Most people had no idea. When the clerk at the grocery store said, "How are you today?" I had to remind myself, "She doesn't know. She doesn't really want to know." When the teller at the bank said, "Have a nice day." I said to myself, "He doesn't know. Remember, he doesn't know."

Part of me wanted to wear a shirt that said, "Please be nice to me. I just lost my son." It's not that people were actually being mean; they were just oblivious. The whole experience gave new meaning to the saying, "Be nice. Everyone around you is facing a battle you don't know."

In the past few lessons, we have learned that God has given Christians freedom from sin and death. He has given us that freedom so that we can live well with God and ourselves. Today's lesson reminds us that we have also been give freedom so that we can live well with others.

Be Humble

In Romans 12, we find several commands to think of ourselves with honesty and humility. Paul reminds us that as Christians, we are all part of the body of Christ. Just like every part of our bodies is important, every person in the body of Christ is a valuable member. We should never consider ourselves better than anyone else.

Be Loving

It's relatively easy to say, "I love you." It's a little harder to show it. Unfortunately, there are some people that are simply harder to love than others. God calls us to love everyone—to really love them—and to make a sincere effort to honor them. Remember, sometimes the most unlovable people are the ones who need love the most.

Be Good

It sounds simple enough, but we all know that it isn't. If we're honest with ourselves, we will admit that sometimes it's fun to be bad—at least for a little while. In this passage, we are reminded that we should always hate what is wrong. Our desire should be to imitate Christ and His goodness and, in that way, to live honorable lives.

Be A Hard Worker

Did you realize that your performance at work matters to God? God says that we should work hard and enthusiastically. That's more than a little convicting. Colossians 3:23 tells us that we should work like we are working for the Lord, not men.

Be Generous And Hospitable

Most Christians realize that God calls us to be generous. Practicing hospitality takes generosity a step further. It means being friendly and welcoming not only to those we know but also to strangers. That's something to think about the next time someone cuts in line at the grocery store.

Be Peaceful

Living at peace is easy when the people around us are peaceful people, right? But interestingly enough, God doesn't ask us to live peacefully with just the people we like. In Romans 12, Paul gives several verses toward the command to live "in harmony" with everyone, including our enemies. He even goes so far as to tell us to bless our enemies and pray for them.

Be Kind

Cry with those who cry and laugh with those who laugh. Notice the verses don't say anything about whether or not you know them. Remember, no matter how a person looks on the outside—the color of their skin, the clothes they wear, the language they speak, the way they act or things they say—we are all humans, and we all need love—God's love and the love of others.

Galatians 5:13-14 says it best. So, I will end this lesson with those words:

"For you have been called to live in freedom, my brothers and sisters. But don't use your freedom to satisfy your sinful nature. Instead, use your freedom to serve one another in love. For the whole law can be summed up in in this one command: 'Love your neighbor as yourself.'"

Notes:

August

What Can We Learn About...?

August Week One

The Problem of Sin and What Can Be Done About It

Read: 1 John 1:7-2:2 and 1 John 3:4-10

Primary Point: The law helps us realize our sinfulness; our sinfulness helps us realize we need a Savior.

Memory Verse: "If we claim we have no sin, we are only fooling ourselves and not living in the truth." *1 John 1:8*

The Problem of Sin and What We Can Do About It

All of my boys gave their hearts to Jesus at young ages. While I recognize the concern about children understanding that decision, I am also keenly aware that the Bible tells us not to forbid little children from coming to Him (Matthew 19:14).

So, when our children expressed an interest in getting saved, Ian and I took it very seriously. We began by asking a series of questions to see how much they knew about salvation and the gospel story. When Brandon approached us about salvation, he had all the right answers. But, Interestingly, however, he balked at the notion of his own sinfulness. Oh, he understood what sin is; actually, he even went so far as to tell all the sins that his brother, Sjon-Paul, committed. However, he was very reluctant to name any of his own!

Sin is funny like that. So many times, it is easy to spot sin in others while it remains elusive in the examination of our own hearts and lives. Perhaps the problem is that we don't actually understand sin or what the Bible has to say about it.

What Is Sin?

1 John 3:4 says, "Everyone who sins is breaking God's law, for all sin is contrary to the law of God." Therefore, sin is break-

ing God's law. The Greek word used here for "sin" literally means "missing the mark." God's law is the mark or bull's eye for which we are aiming.

Of course, we find God's law in the Bible. The Bible is God's Word, and, as the author of the Bible, God is, therefore, the authority on sin. If we break God's law, we are missing the mark; we are sinning. If you know anything about the Bible, you will understand that there are many different "laws" in it. Even if we narrow it down to just the most popular ten commandments, it is impossible to keep all of them. This leads us to the next point.

Who Is A Sinner?

Everyone sins. *Most people probably recognize this and don't even try to argue. Just in case, take a look at 1 John 1:8 and 10, "If we claim we have no sin, we are only fooling ourselves and not living in the truth...If we claim we have not sinned, we are calling God a liar and showing that His word has no place in our hearts."

Based on these verses, it is not possible that even the best person in the world is sinless. Why? Because God's laws aren't just about what we <u>do or don't do</u>. They also address what we say and what we think. They apply to our motives and intentions as well as our actions. In other words, sinning is just as much a matter of the heart and mind as it is the body.

Why Does Sin Matter?

Sin puts us in opposition to others and God. Our sinful human nature demands that we take care of ourselves—our own needs, wants, and wishes—above all else. Thinking about this, it is easy to see how we wind up offending one another. It doesn't take long for my rights to impose upon your rights or vice versa. More importantly, the Bible also tells us that as sinners we are placing ourselves in direct opposition to the Creator of all things and in alliance with His greatest opponent, Satan.

1 John 3:8 says, "But when people keep on sinning, it shows that they belong to the devil who has been sinning since the beginning. But the Son of God came to destroy the works of the devil."

If we are doing 80 in a 55 MPH zone, and the police pull us over, we understand that we have broken the law; there is going to be a price to pay. By breaking the law, we have put ourselves in opposition to the those who create and enforce the law. Just like there are penalties for breaking the laws in our country, there are penalties for breaking God's law.

The price for sin is greater than any penalty imposed upon us for breaking man's law. Romans 6:23 tells us that sin earns death. This death is not just physical death but an eternal separation from God.

Is There Any Good News About Sin?

Let's just admit it. We all know that sometimes sin *is* fun, at least for a while. This makes things sound rather grim. After all, based on what we have learned, sin is inevitable. It is impossible <u>not</u> to sin, but there are terrible consequences for sinning. It really seems unfair, like we are set up for failure. If that is the case, why should we even try? Why should we even worry about any of this?

Here is the Good News. In fact, it is the best news you will ever hear. God doesn't leave us in our sinfulness. He also doesn't expect us to clear it up on our own. He doesn't want us to try to earn our way to Him by being good enough. In fact, while living by God's law has earthly benefits, the primary purpose of the law is to help us recognize that we can't fulfill it on our own.

The Law Makes Us Realize Our Sinfulness. Our Sinfulness Helps Us Realize That We Need A Savior.

1 John 1:9 says, "If we confess our sins to Him, He is faithful and just to forgive us our sins and to cleanse us from all wickedness." 1 John 2:1(b)-2 says, "we have an advocate who pleads our case before the Father. He is Jesus Christ, the one who is truly righteous. He Himself is the sacrifice that atones for our sins—and not only our sins but the sins of all the world." 1 John 3:5 says, "And you know that Jesus came to take away our sins, and there is no sin in Him."

Jesus Christ, the Son of God, the only sinless human to have ever lived, paid the price for our sin. It is only through Him that we can find forgiveness for our sins and align ourselves with God. He is the Savior that we all need.

Although Brandon didn't understand everything about sin, he eventually came to understand enough. Not too many months after that initial conversation, Brandon was ready to confess his own sinfulness. He then asked God to forgive him and received the free gift of salvation offered through the sacrifice of Jesus Christ.

Of course, this isn't an exhaustive study on sin. There is always more to learn; so, again, I encourage you to study God's Word for yourself. The Bible has lots more to say about this and all of the subjects we have studied thus far. Don't take my word for it, take a look! God wants to speak to you!

---

*Some people will argue that not everyone sins because, after all, babies don't sin. I would agree—and disagree. Infants do not physically commit sin, but they are born with the capacity to do so and will as soon as they begin to make any choices on their own. Ask any parent if they had to teach their children to do wrong. Since our human in-

stinct is self-protection, self-preservation, and self-promotion, even the kindest, most sweet-natured children have to be taught to do what is right and not to do what is wrong. To say that an infant is not a sinner because they haven't yet sinned is like saying that a bald infant is not a mammal because he or she does not yet have hair.

Notes:

August Week Two

What Does it Mean to be Saved?

Read: Romans 3:9-28

Primary Point: Because of sin, we're sinking, but we can be saved.

Memory Verse: "If you openly declare that Jesus is Lord and believe in your heart that God raised him from the dead, you will be saved. For it is by believing in your heart that you are made right with God, and it is by openly declaring your faith that you are saved." *Romans 10:9-10*

What Does It Mean to Be Saved?

In my in-law's house there is a painting. The painting shows a great chasm. On one side is a dark, urban background. On the other side is a bright, lush landscape. Bridging the chasm is a cross. It's not my favorite painting, but it is one that has often caught my eye because it represents salvation.

Salvation is one of those churchy words. You hear it often in religious circles. As Christians, we use the term to describe the process of placing one's faith in Jesus Christ. Therefore, it is essential to the message of Christianity. Yet, if you asked even seasoned believers, you might find them stumbling over a definition. Sometimes it's harder to explain things than it is to understand them. If we truly have a relationship with Christ, then it is important that we know how to talk about it. If we want to see others come to Jesus, we must be able to explain how. So, let's see what we can learn about salvation.

What Is Salvation? Romans 3:10-20

Let's start with a non-Biblical answer. Salvation comes from the term "save" which means to be delivered from harm. Literally, salvation is the act of being delivered from harm.

There must be an element of danger in order to need saving or delivering. In Christianity, salvation is the act of being saved from sin and its eternal consequences. While the consequences of sin can be as varied as the sins themselves, the final and most severe consequence of sin is a death that leads to eternal separation from God in hell.

Why does sin have such dire consequences? I can only tell you what the Bible tells us. God is our Creator, and as such, He gets to make the rules. He is our ultimate authority. He is holy, perfectly clean. Sin is unholy, dirty. God cannot abide sin. Therefore, sinners are condemned to eternally live apart from God.

Who Is In Danger? Romans 3:23

As we discussed in last week's lesson, everyone is a sinner. Since sin is a part of our human nature, we are all born sinners, and, therefore, we are all in danger. We can, of course, suffer the consequences of our sins during our lifetime here on earth. While, by human standards, some people behave "better" than others and may, therefore, live with fewer consequences, all sinners (apart from being saved) will face the final consequence of an eternity in hell after death.

What Can We Do About It? Romans 3:21-23

The Bible tells us that we cannot do anything to save ourselves. In addition, we cannot save each other. Although that's hard for some people to accept, the Bible tells us that no amount of good deeds will help. It doesn't matter how often we go to church or how much we give to charity. I can't help you, and you can't help me because none of us are perfect; none of us are holy. We are in the same boat, and it's sinking. We all need to be saved.

Who Can Save Us? Romans 3:24-26

In the case of Christianity, salvation is the act of being delivered from sin and its consequences. If we can't help ourselves or each other, who can save us? God loved us enough not to leave us in condemnation. So, He sent His Son, Jesus, to be born as a human, to live a perfect, sinless life, and to pay the consequences for our sins (John 3:16).

How Does A Person "Get Saved"? Romans 3:27-28

Because Jesus was the Only One who was able to live among humanity without sin, He is the Only One who can help pull us out of this mess. Because the consequence of sin is death, Jesus paid that price for us. He died for us on the cross, and then He rose again, defeating death. Through Him, and Him alone, we can be rescued from sin, death, and eternal damnation.

If we live our lives believing that everything is OK, that we don't need saving, then we will die in our sinful condition. So, the first step to salvation is admitting one's own sinfulness and need for a Savior. The second step is believing that there is only One who can do the saving, and His name is Jesus Christ. The third step is confessing all this to Jesus and placing faith in Him.

Of course, salvation is not just a one-time prayer. Salvation is not a "Get Out of Hell Free" card to carry in your pocket. Salvation is not something you do on a Sunday morning and forget on Monday. Salvation is heart-changing and life-changing.

Imagine you are caught in a rip tide, with a storm brewing above you, and currents of cold water pulling you under the waves. Imagine you are struggling to stay afloat and feel yourself drowning fast. Then, the lifeguard comes to rescue you. He pulls you out of the water, wraps a blanket around your shivering frame, and starts to take you home. What do you do? Do you tell him that you just want to wade in a little to feel the rush of the ocean against your legs one more time? Do you ask him to wait a minute while you go skinny-dipping for a while? Do you jump back in and expect him to rescue you all over again?

Salvation is a free gift to us. God loves us enough to make a way to Him. Jesus loves us enough to pay for our sins. It's all by grace that we are saved (Ephesians 2:8-9), but that doesn't mean we should take our salvation for granted. It doesn't mean we should wallow around in the same sin that Jesus rescued us from. Until we reach our eternal home with Christ, we, as Christians, will not be perfect, and thank God, He doesn't expect us to be. However, out of love and respect for the One who rescued us, we should strive to live in a way that is pleasing to Him.

Jesus bridges the chasm between us and God. He provides a way to escape certain damnation and to experience life in Christ. God loves me and you enough that He sent His Son to die for us. My prayer is that You have already experienced the work of salvation in your heart and life. If so, I hope that this lesson serves as a reminder and maybe a tool to help you share the message with others. If you still haven't taken this step, then I pray you don't wait. We are never guaranteed a tomorrow.

Notes:

August Week Three

Angels Aren't Really in the Outfield, or Are They?

Read: Hebrews 1

Primary Point: Angels are servants not the Savior.

Memory Verse: "Jesus replied, 'The Scriptures say, "You must worship the Lord your God and serve only him."'" *Luke 4:8*

Angels Aren't Really in the Outfield—or Are They?

Like the previous two subjects we have studied, the study of angels cannot be relegated to a short devotional. Therefore, I highly recommend that you study God's Word to discover more about the spirit world, including angels.

In both Hebrew and Greek, the words used for angels means messengers. In the Bible, they are sometimes referenced by different words, including (but not limited to) "the host," "host of Heaven," or "Heavenly host," as well as "sons of God," "sons of the mighty," "holy ones," "heavenly beings," and "living beings."

Despite the cute little cherub pictures, we see on Valentine's Day cards, the Bible does not give the indication that angels look like chubby babies with wings. In fact, some angelic descriptions are quite exceptional and fearsome (See Revelation 4). While television shows like *Highway to Heaven* and *Touched by an Angel* did much to promote quality, family-friendly fiction, the way in which angels are portrayed in the media today does little to promote the actual truth about these spiritual beings.

Due to space limitations, I am going to limit our study to only a few Biblical facts about angels that may surprise you.

Our Loved Ones In Heaven Do Not Become Angels.

Despite how frequently you hear this reference, it is not Biblical. This mistaken belief may have originated from Matthew 22:29-30 which states, "For when the dead rise, they will neither marry nor be given in marriage. In this respect, they will be like the angels in heaven."

Some versions are less clear, but Jesus's intent here was to answer a question that had been posed to Him in regards to marriage in Heaven. He was, therefore, stating that in Heaven, the redeemed would be like angels in this one respect—not marrying. It was not to say that we would become angels. Since the way we interpret scripture is always by using other scripture, let's unpack this more.

Angels are created beings. While we aren't exactly sure when angels were created, we know that they were here before mankind. In Job 38:4-7, God asks Job, "Where were you when I laid the foundations of the earth...as the morning stars sang together and all the angels shouted for joy?" In addition, angels are as different from humans as cats are from dogs. If we were to become angels, God would literally have to change us from one being into another. Of course, nothing is impossible with God, but this seems unlikely.

The Bible clearly states that in Heaven, humans will be over angels. In 1 Corinthians 6:2-3(a) we read, "Don't you realize that someday we believers will judge the world...Don't you realize that we will judge angels?" This would be an odd statement for Paul to make if human believers died and became angels.

In addition, Hebrews 2:16 states, "We also know that the Son did not come to help angels; he came to help the descendants of Abraham." Salvation through Jesus Christ was only offered to humans. It is a special privilege to which the angels have no access. So, while there may be similarities that we will share, the Bible offers clear evidence that believers do not become angels when we die. That's more than OK because Romans 8:17 calls us God's heirs. So, don't be disappointed that your loved one is not an angel. In Heaven, Christians are more than just servants in God's house; they are co-heirs with Christ!

Angels Have A Variety Of Jobs, Some Of Which May Surprise You.

Let's just go ahead and say it. There is nothing in scripture that indicates angels play Cupid. While they may not carry little bows and arrows dipped in love potion, they do a lot of other things. As their name suggests, they often serve as messengers for God. Think about the messages that Mary, Joseph, and Zechariah received from angels.

However, they are also warriors and military leaders. In Daniel 10, an angel appears to Daniel in answer to a prayer. Speaking to Daniel, the angel explained that he was delayed because a demon commander (a fallen angel) opposed him for 21 days. When the angel left, he told Daniel that he was returning to fight. Given these and other scriptures, invisible battles are probably going on around us every day.

In addition to serving as messengers and warriors, angels have other jobs as well. As you might expect, they worship and praise God. They carry out His judgments, and they minister to and protect God's people. In 1 Kings 19:7, an angel wakes a very depressed and despondent Elijah, provides food and water, and tells him to eat and drink.

Angels Can Take On Human Form.

There are many times in the Bible when angels appeared in some sort of physical form, thus indicating that angels can indeed take on human form when God so directs. In addition, Hebrews 13:1-2 says, "Keep on loving each other as brothers and sisters. Don't forget to show hospitality to strangers, for some who have done this have entertained angels without realizing it!" So, according to this scripture, we can assume that we may have even seen or spoken to an angel without realizing it.

However, just to be clear, when angels appeared to humans in the Bible it was usually unexpected and unrequested. While angels are on this earth performing purposes for which God sends them, I would venture to say that the majority of time, we have no idea of their presence. This brings me to my last point.

Angels Are Not To Be Prayed To Or Worshiped.

Sometimes in our zeal for spiritual awareness, we can take things too far. Such is the case with angels. Angels seem to have developed a following all their own. As Christians, we must be very cautious and very clear. As stated earlier, angels are part of creation—just like this earth, just like us. They are not self-existing. They are not omnipresent (everywhere at once). They are not omniscient (knowing everything). In Luke 4:8, quoting one of the ten commandments, Jesus said, "You must worship the Lord your God and serve only him." Angels are spiritual creatures that God made to do His will. As such, they should not be prayed to (a form of worship) or worshipped in any other way.

In Romans 1:25, the writer warns against this and other forms of false worship when he writes, "They traded the truth about God for a lie. So, they worshiped and served the things God created instead of the Creator himself, who is worthy of eternal praise! Amen."

In Revelation 22:8-9, John is admonished for making this very mistake. "I John," he writes, "am the one who heard and saw all these things. And, when I heard and saw them, I fell down to worship at the feet of the angel who showed them to me. The angel said, 'No, don't worship me. I am a servant of God, just like you and your brothers the prophets, as well as all who obey what is written in this book. Worship only God!'"

If all that isn't clear enough, you can read how Paul, when advising new Christians about how to live in the freedom of Christ, warns them, "Don't let anyone condemn you by insisting on pious self-denial or the worship of angels..." (1 Colossians 2:18-19)

Angels are, obviously, fascinating. If you want to learn the truth about who they are and what they do, don't turn to popular culture. Turn to God's Word. When you dig in, you will find that the Bible is full of drama, adventure, love, and mystery. Spend some time exploring His Word this week.

Notes:

August Week Four

Ten Things You May Not Know About Heaven

Read: Revelation 4 and 21

Primary Point: Christians have a home prepared for them in Heaven.

Memory Verse: "He will wipe every tear from their eyes, and there will be no more death or sorrow or crying or pain. All these things are gone forever." *Revelation 21:4*

Ten Things You May Not Know About Heaven

I have a confession to make. I never thought about Heaven as much as I have since Brandon died. I don't think I have ever really desired Heaven as much either. I have asked Jesus to forgive me for that. After all, shouldn't my heart long to see my Savior much more than I long to see my son? Still, God is good and gracious, and, along with His forgiveness, He has used my new-found desire to teach me many things about eternity. There is no way to share everything with you here. So, I have decided to key in on 10 things you may not know about Heaven. This is just a starting point. Remember, this is to pique your interest not to quench it.

Heaven Is A Real Place.

CS Lewis wrote, "Heaven is not a state of mind. Heaven is reality itself."[4]

Of course, we don't have to take CS Lewis's word for it. We know Heaven is a real, physical place because the Bible tells us so. Throughout scripture we frequently read of physical things in Heaven (a temple, a throne, horses, trees, etc.). While some of these may be spiritual representations, it is doubtful that they all are. Why would God tell us all about the things in Heaven if Heaven were only a state of mind?

Heaven Is God's Home.

While we may not know where exactly Heaven is located, we do know Who lives there. The Lord's Prayer (Matthew 6) begins with "Our Father, who art in Heaven..." and Colossians 3:1 tells us that Christ is seated at His right hand. As believers, this should be our greatest comfort, knowing that God our Father and Jesus our Savior are waiting to welcome us home when we die.

Heaven Is Not The Christian's Eternal Home.

That one may have caught you by surprise. Revelation 21 and other scriptures tell us that ultimately God will recreate earth in a Heavenly fashion. Therefore, a new and perfect earth will be our final destination (Revelation 21).

We Will Work In Heaven.

Yes, there will be rest in Heaven, but we won't sit around on clouds playing harps for all of eternity. Revelation 7:15 tells us directly that those in Heaven will serve God. Other places in scripture from Genesis onward highlight the value of work. There is no reason to believe that God will change His opinion on that in eternity. Don't worry, work in Heaven will, like everything else, be pure joy.

We Will Learn In Heaven.

Contrary to popular belief, we will not know everything in Heaven. Revelations 6:10 gives evidence to that fact. In that passage the martyred saints ask God a question. If they can ask questions, it can be assumed that they don't have all the answers themselves. Just imagine! We can ask Moses to describe what it was like to walk across the parted Red Sea. We can talk to Lazarus about his first death. Our minds, unhindered by the curse of sin, will be able to comprehend subjects and learn skills that were beyond our abilities in our natural bodies.

We Will Remember Our Lives On Earth.

In Revelation 6, the saints remembered the cruelties done to them. The story of the rich man and Lazarus the beggar in Luke 16:19-31 also indicates the ability to remember our previous lives after death. Even though we will remember our former lives, we will not be tormented by them, no matter how grim they may have been, and we will not miss them, no matter how wonderful they may now seem. Randy Alcorn, author of the comprehensive book Heaven, writes, "Heaven's happiness won't be dependent on our ignorance of what happened on Earth. Rather, it will be enhanced by our informed appreciation of God's glorious grace and justice as we grasp what really happened here."[5] Our joy will not be fleeting because it will not be a product of circumstances but of a perfect, Godly perspective.

We Will Know One Another.

Jesus and the disciples recognized Moses and Elijah on the Mount of Transfiguration (Luke 9:28-36). With the exception of the Emmaus Road where He kept Himself from being recognized, Jesus Himself was recognized after His own death and resurrection. 1 Thessalonians 4:13-18 is an encouragement to believers who have lost loved ones, but it wouldn't be much of an encouragement if we aren't going to recognize our loved ones in Heaven. While our hearts will be full of love for everyone, we will remember and know those we hold dear in our earthly lives.

Heaven Will Be Fun.

There seems to be a misconception that only sinful things bring pleasure, but the Bible tells us that all good things come from God (James 1:17). While Heaven will be absent of sin and evil (Praise the Lord!), it will be full of laughter, love, and fun. We can be assured that the God who created pleasure will also include it in His Home.

Everyone Will Not Be In Heaven.

Revelation 21:27 is a harsh reminder that not everyone will live in eternity with God. "Nothing evil will be allowed to enter, nor anyone who practices shameful idolatry and dishonesty—but only those whose names are written in the Lamb's Book of Life." Joshua 24:15 reminds us that there is a choice to make. Heaven is God's Home, and God will not welcome those Who have not chosen Him.

Just in case there is any misunderstanding, we don't get to choose the road to God. In John 14:6 Jesus says, "I am the way, the truth, and the life. No one can come to the Father except through me." We are sinners, and God is not. He is holy, perfect, and completely righteous. He requires righteousness from us. Of course, that is something we cannot attain in and of ourselves. No matter how "good" any of us think we are, if we are honest, we would admit that we are not perfect. We are sinners, but Jesus, who lived and died a perfect man, paid the price for us. Through Him, we have a way to spend eternity with God.

If there is any doubt whether you have a saving relationship with our Lord and Savior, I beg you not to wait. You don't want to miss out on the peace and comfort of living with Him today or the joy of living with Him in eternity.

God Wants Us To Think About Heaven.

Study God's Word about Heaven. It's even OK to use your divine imagination. Just like a parent awaiting his child's return from a long trip, God wants us to make the most of our time here, but He is also looking forward to the day we will come home. We should think about Heaven with love and anticipation as well.

Notes:

August Week Five

The Alternative to Heaven is Hell—
Not Somewhere You Want to Go

Read: Luke 16:19-31

Primary Point: Jesus is the way to Heaven. Without Him, the alternative is Hell.

Memory Verse: "The Lord isn't really being slow about his promise, as some people think. No, he is being patient for your sake. He does not want anyone to be destroyed, but wants everyone to repent." *2 Peter 3:9*

The Alternative to Heaven is Hell— Not Somewhere You Want to Go

Special Note: This is a serious subject. Please don't take my introduction as frivolity. It's funny, but it's meant to make a point. If there was one subject that I could avoid writing about, this would be it. I don't know anyone who wants to think about hell. But, let's be absolutely clear, hell is just as real as Heaven. So, we need to know about it. We need to understand how people wind up there, because many have already, and many more will.

I do not claim to know everything there is on this subject or on any other. I am not a theologian. Therefore, I have included many scriptures where this information has been found. I want you to understand that these aren't my opinions. The points I included here have been gleaned from scripture. However, it is my sincere desire that you don't just take my word for it. Use this lesson as a starting point for further study. God wants each individual to study His Word and learn what He has to say on these topics and many others. If you have any questions, I would be happy to assist in any way that I can.

There were two wicked brothers who, despite living like the devil, often donated from their extensive wealth to the church and other charities. Finally, one of the brothers passed away, and the preacher was asked to speak at the funeral. Before the service, the surviving brother handed the preacher an envelope and said, "Inside that envelope is a check large enough to ensure that the church never has a cash problem again." The preacher was intrigued, but the brother continued. "All you have to do is tell that audience that my brother was a saint."

Downcast, the preacher pondered what to do. The church needed the money, but he realized he couldn't lie. Finally, he took the money and agreed to the terms. Later that day, with the sanctuary full of people, he looked out over the man's casket and said with confidence, "This man was an evil, wicked, reprobate, but compared to his brother, he was a saint."

It's a comical story to be sure, but make no mistake. There is a lot of truth there. Our world has some funny ideas about salvation and how we get to Heaven. Unfortunately, those views directly impact what we think about hell. The truth is simple.

Everyone Will Not Be In Heaven.

You can't buy your way to Heaven. You can't work your way to Heaven. No preacher can talk you into Heaven by saying nice things at your funeral. The only way you can get to Heaven is by having a personal relationship with Jesus Christ.

Only God Can Cast People Into Hell.

It may be a popular curse phrase, but no one can send anyone to damnation. Matthew 10:28 and Luke 12:5 tell us clearly that only God has the power and authority to cast anyone into hell.

Hell Wasn't Created For Humans.

God didn't originally create hell for human beings. In Matthew 25:41 we read that hell was created for Satan and the angels who chose to follow Satan in rebellion.

God Doesn't Want Anyone To Go To Hell.

Despite the opinions of those who think God is just itching to reign fire and brimstone, the Bible tells us that God loves us. He truly wants us to know and love Him. 2 Peter 3:9 says, "The Lord isn't really being slow about his promise, as some people think. No, he is being patient for your sake. He does not want anyone to be destroyed, but wants everyone to repent." Anyone who winds up in hell does so because he or she refuses God's love. God will not make you choose Him. Think of it like this. I can buy you a ticket to a paradise vacation, but I can't make you get on the plane. Jesus has paid the price for our sin; He has made the way for you to go to Heaven. If you refuse to accept His gift, then you won't get there. The only alternative to Heaven is hell.

Hell Will Not Be A Party.

Based on at least one story that Jesus told (Luke 16:19-31), we have reason to believe there is cognition and possibly even conversations in hell, but there will not be any pleasure in hell. Hell, in its most basic form, is an absence of God. Since everything good comes from God (including the ability to experience pleasure), we can be sure that there won't be anything pleasant in hell. There will be no joy, no hope, and no peace. In multiple places in God's Word, including Mark 9:43-49, hell is described as a place of fire and eternal burning. Those who think that hell will be a place to gather with their friends for an indulgently wicked party are sadly mistaken.

Hell Is Forever.

Humans were made for eternity. Therefore, just like Heaven, hell is forever. Hebrews 6:2 refers to "eternal judgment," and Mathew 25:46 refers to "eternal punishment." In Luke 16:19-31, Jesus tells a story of an unnamed rich man and a poor man named Lazarus (not the Lazarus who was raised from the dead). In the story, both the rich man and the poor man die. The rich man went to "Hades" or "the place of the dead" where he was in torment. The poor man, however, was "carried by the angels to sit beside Abraham at the heavenly banquet." At some point the rich man looked up and asked Abraham to let Lazarus dip his finger in water and cool his burning tongue. Abraham replied that no one can cross over the chasm that separated them. Then the rich man begged Abraham to send Lazarus to his family "so they don't end up in this place of torment." Despite all the warnings his family may have already received, the rich man was convinced that his family would turn to God if someone came to them back from the dead. Abraham believed otherwise.

The story has nothing to do with being rich or poor. It's really about those last few sentences. If you have loved ones who have died without Jesus, if you think they are more than likely in hell, remember this. Very seldom do we know what is truly happening in the hearts and minds of our loved ones at the point of death. We can hope that in their final breaths they said "yes" to Christ. Still, I am confident that if there is someone you know who is in hell today, if they could speak to you now, they would urge you not to make the same mistake they made.

You see, someone did come back from the dead. That someone is Jesus Christ. 1 Corinthians 15:2-4 says, "It is this Good News that saves you if you continue to believe the message I told you… Christ died for our sins, just as the Scriptures said. He was buried, and he was raised from the dead on the third day, just as the Scriptures said." John 3:16 tells us that God sent His Son, Jesus, to die for us so that by believing in Him we can avoid hell and instead have everlasting life.

You can't buy your way into Heaven. You can't work your way into Heaven. You can't wish your way into Heaven or have the preacher preach you into Heaven. The Bible makes it abundantly clear that there is only one way to Heaven—through

God's Son, Jesus Christ. If you don't know Him, then you won't go to Heaven, and the alternative is hell.

Please consider carefully where you are headed. I am praying for you.

Notes:

September

A Life of Faith—Learning from Elijah

September Week One

Relying on God's Provision

Read: 1 Kings 17:1-16

Primary Point: God doesn't promise it will be easy, but He promises that He will provide.

Memory Verse: "And this same God who takes care of me will supply all your needs from his glorious riches, which have been given to us in Christ Jesus." *Philippians 4:19*

Relying on God's Provision

I knew that Brandon was gone before the police officer arrived at our door. Still, when I saw him walk down our front hall, carrying my son's backpack in his hands, an overwhelming and irrational sense of anger rose inside me. Pointing at him, I said, "I don't want to talk to him!"

It's our human nature to blame the news-bearer, even if he had no part in the news. Thus, the saying, "Don't shoot the messenger."

That must have been heavy on Elijah's mind as he delivered God's words to the wicked King Ahab. "There will be no rain for the next few years."

Rain, as we all know, is vital to our very existence, and in a time without modern irrigation techniques, a drought was deadly. So, it's very likely that Ahab didn't take the news well. Knowing that he was at least partially responsible wouldn't have helped matters at all.

Because God knew Ahab's temperament, He sent Elijah into hiding as soon as the prophet delivered the fateful news. There, Elijah learned that a life of faith requires a reliance on God's provision. Let's examine how that looked for Elijah and what it means for us as well.

Obedience Doesn't Always Result In A Favorable Outcome.

Somehow, we have the impression that if we are "good," we will be rewarded. Like obedient children, we almost demand our treats. Elijah was obedient; he did what God asked him to do. King Ahab and his notoriously evil wife, Jezebel, did not give him a reward for the heads-up. In fact, they were more likely to ask for his head on a platter! Though obedience is a necessary product of faith, obedience does not always result in a favorable outcome—at least not on this earth. Just because we do what God tells us to do does not mean that we will live a life free of trouble. Like Elijah, we should understand that obedience is sometimes dangerous.

God's Provision Doesn't Always Look Pretty.

God provided for Elijah, but maybe not in the way he had hoped. No one put Elijah up in a five-star hotel with room service. Instead, God sent him to a remote area to camp out. Instead of receiving dinner from a silver spoon, he collected meat scraps from birds that were considered unclean. When it was time to move on, God then sent him to a widow. If you are picturing a saintly little old grandma rocking on her front porch sipping a glass of lemonade, I better set you straight. Elijah was sent to Zarephath, near the city of Sidon, Jezebel's hometown! Then, to beat it all, the widow was as hungry as Elijah—maybe more so since she had a son for whom she had been caring and no ravens dropping off dinner. Of course, God did provide, but here's a lesson for us. God's provision doesn't always look like we might picture it.

God's Contribution May Be Directly Related To Our Compliance.

Elijah once again obeyed God. He went where he was told despite the fact that he must have felt like he walking straight into the hornet's nest. He found the widow, and he asked her for water and a bite to eat. It didn't take long for him to learn about her predicament. Does he say, "Oh, I am so sorry. I must have the wrong widow. I will ask someone else." Does he offer to pray with her or give her directions to the local food closet? No, he says, "OK, well, go ahead and fix your last meal, but make me something to eat first." Then, he assured her that the Lord would provide for her needs. Did I mention that this widow lived in a <u>foreign</u> land, a land known for its worship of pagan gods? We have the benefit of knowing the end of the story, but she didn't. What if she had said, "No, thank you, sir. If I make food for you, I won't have enough for even one last meal for me and my son. I'm sorry about your luck. I really am, but you are on your own. If I happen to have any leftovers, I will be happy to give them to you after we eat."

Instead, though, the widow chose to trust and obey; then, she personally experienced God's provision, not just for one meal or one day or even one week. In fact, the passage says, "There was <u>always enough</u> flour and olive oil left in the containers" (v. 16).

Sometimes, how much God contributes to our needs may be directly related to how well we comply with His instructions.

Living a life of faith means obeying regardless of the outcome, being thankful even when the provision isn't pretty, and complying with God's instructions even if they seem to defy common sense. God doesn't promise it will be easy, but He does promise that He will provide.

Notes:

September Week Two

Relying on God's Protection

Read: 1 Kings 18

Primary Point: A life of faith requires a certain amount of fearlessness.

Memory Verse: "And when all the people saw it, they fell face down on the ground and cried out, 'The Lord—he is God! Yes, the Lord is God!'" *1 Kings 18:39*

Relying on God's Protection

What is the most daring thing you've ever done? Me? I can't think of anything—nope, nothing really adventurous. I'm not a risk taker. In fact, I'm quite the scaredy-cat.

I am not one to enjoy fast rides or thrilling adventures. For the most part, I'm much more content with routine and stability. I guess you can say that I'm rather boring, a complete contrast to many heroes of faith. If you look at the lives of Old Testament prophets, like Elijah, and New Testament saints, like Paul, you'll find that boring is not an adjective that adequately describes them or their ministries.

In our last lesson, Elijah informed the wicked king and queen that there would be a severe drought. Knowing that this drought was God's punishment and understanding their own evil natures, King Ahab and Queen Jezebel didn't take the news well. So, God sent Elijah into hiding where God miraculously provided for Elijah's needs.

In today's lesson, God called Elijah out of hiding and sends him back to the king to report that rain is now on the way. While the message is good, Elijah is no dummy. He understands that Ahab still blames him for the drought in the first place. So, we can only imagine the fear that must have been present as Elijah obediently started on his trip. It was certainly evident in the demeanor of the prophet, Obadiah, who Elijah met on the way.

Elijah and Obadiah, as well as all of the other prophets and Christ followers in the Bible, were human—just like us. It's easy to forget that sometimes. We read their stories, and we begin to fictionalize them. We give them superhuman abilities that they simply did not have. That's why I love Obadiah's response to Elijah in this passage.

Obadiah was a Godly man, but he had witnessed the king and queen's wickedness up close. He had even put his own life on the line to keep other prophets safe. However, he didn't want to report Elijah's arrival to the king. He knew that there was no guarantee. You can sense his fear as he argued with Elijah. He realized the risk.

We who live in North America celebrate a certain amount of liberty to worship as we please. As such, it's easy for us to forget that there is risk involved with our faith. Just because we follow God's commands, just because we are obedient, it does not mean that we won't face danger. God does not guarantee safety and safe passage on this earth. A quick look at the lives and deaths of the disciples will confirm the point. Even today, there are millions of Christians who have been and continue to be martyred for their faith.

The sacrifices that Christians are called to make today vary in great degrees, but the principle is still the same for us all.

God's Defense Doesn't Negate Our Need To Be Daring.

Being a Christian takes courage. As I was preparing this lesson, I heard a news report about a young girl named Leah Sharibu.* In February, 2018, Leah was one of 110 girls kidnapped by the Boko Haram, a Nigerian terrorist group. Every girl except Leah was eventually released. Leah was kept hostage because she refused to renounce her faith in Christ. She was 14 at the time and has since celebrated several birthdays.

Doing God's Will Can Be Dangerous.

It was for Elijah. It was for Obadiah. It was for Leah. Can you imagine? I cannot. I hope, I pray, that should I ever face a similar situation, I will have the kind of courage that Leah Sharibu has, the kind of courage that Elijah and Obadiah had.

Not only did Elijah confront the king, he confronted him with boldness. "You and your family are the troublemakers," he said. Then he requested that the king gather everyone, including the prophets of Baal and Asherah, together. Do you understand the seriousness of that request? As if facing the King wasn't bad enough, he was asking for more trouble—hundreds of the enemies of God in one place. Basically, Elijah was calling them to a showdown.

On this side of history, knowing the outcome, reading the story in the safety of our own homes, it's easy to miss the danger that was present. Elijah was definitely in the minority at this gathering. He would have been considered an enemy of the state. He could have easily been lynched. Still, he moved forward with confidence.

It's one of my favorite stories in the Bible. If this doesn't show God's sense of humor, I'm not sure what does. Elijah told the false prophets to erect an altar and a sacrifice to Baal, and they did so. Elijah said, "Don't light it. Let your god do that for you." So, all day, the prophets danced and called out to their god. They shouted. They cried. The begged. They cut themselves to no avail.

"You'll have to shout louder," Elijah shouted. "Perhaps he is daydreaming or is relieving himself. Or maybe he is away on a trip or is asleep and needs to be awakened."

Nothing happened.

So, finally, Elijah prepared for the usual evening sacrifice —with a little twist. He soaked the wood and the sacrifice and even filled a trench around the altar with water. Elijah didn't want there to be any mistake in Who was going to set this fire. Then, he called on the Lord, and God sent a fire that consumed it all—even the stones and the dust.

I wonder if Elijah knew when he started out that day the way in which God was going to use him. The Bible just says that God told Elijah to present himself to the king and to tell him that there would soon be rain. If God said anything about such a combustible climax, the Bible didn't let us in on the secret. I kind of think that it was a surprise to Elijah as well.

How God Uses Us Will Often Be Unanticipated.

Elijah followed the promptings of the Lord, and the Lord took care of the rest. I can't imagine. I really can't. I can't imagine being Elijah. I can't imagine boldly confronting a wicked king. I can't imagine challenging 850 false prophets and all of their followers. I can't imagine standing there in front of them and calling on the Lord for divine intervention.

I can't imagine having the courage to stand up for my faith, knowing that it means captivity or even death. But a life of faith is not a boring life.

A Life Of Faith Requires A Certain Amount Of Fearlessness.

When God called Elijah, Elijah went. Elijah relied on God for provision, and God provided. Elijah relied on God for protection, and God protected. Does it always work out that way? Do the God-followers always get the victory?

No, at least not on this earth. If it did, then Leah Sharibu would be safe at home with her family in Nigeria instead of held captive by terrorists.

Remember, Elijah escaped the wicked King Ahab and Queen Jezebel unharmed, but many Godly prophets did not.

Make no mistake. Faith is not the <u>promise</u> of provision or the <u>promise</u> of protection. Living a life of faith involves a <u>reliance</u> on God for provision and protection that only He can give—whether He chooses to or not. With God, we <u>will be</u> victorious but not necessarily on this earth. That's a tough lesson to swallow. It's an even tougher lesson to live.

*As of January, 2020, Leah Sharibu was still alive and still being held by her captors.[6]

Notes:

September Week Three

Relying on God for Peace

Read: 1 Kings 19

Primary Point: A life of faith means relying on God for peace even in the midst of problems.

Memory Verse: "I am leaving you with a gift—peace of mind and heart. And the peace I give is a gift the world cannot give. So, don't be troubled or afraid." *John 14:27*

Relying on God for Peace

There is a story about a man who went to see a doctor regarding his feelings of depression. The doctor, feeling as if the man simply needed to experience some fun and enjoyment in life, prescribed a trip to the circus. "There is a clown there," the doctor said. "He has the audience rolling in the aisles every night. I'm sure he will make you laugh, and you will be cured from your sadness."

"No," the man said, shaking his head, "He cannot help me. You see, I am the clown."

At the time of this writing, it is suicide prevention month. In the past few weeks, I have personally heard about two suicides. A 14-year-old girl shot herself after her father took away her phone, and a prominent pastor and mental health advocate lost his battle with depression and took his own life. In the past year, there have been many others.

Even Christ-followers suffer from feelings of despondency. A life of faith does not mean that you will not experience fear. A life of faith does not mean that you won't be sad. A life of faith does not make you immune to depression and other forms of mental illness. No one is immune. If you don't believe me, just look at the life of Elijah.

Elijah had just experienced an amazing victory. God won the showdown with the prophets of Baal. God showed up in a big way, proved Himself, and vindicated Elijah. Then, the rain came, and the drought ended. God even granted Elijah temporary super speed to race ahead of the weather and King Ahab's chariot. However, it didn't take long for the tide to turn—again. King Ahab reported everything to Queen Jezebel—including the death of the prophets of Baal. She responded as any evil queen would. She once again threatened Elijah's life.

Elijah started running again. When he finally sat down, he was spent. He had experienced enough. He was tired physically, mentally, emotionally, and spiritually. He prayed, "I have had enough, Lord. Take my life."

Did you hear that? The mighty prophet Elijah wanted to die. He wasn't depressed because he had done something wrong. Elijah obeyed God. He wasn't depressed because he doubted God's power. He experienced first-hand the miraculous provision, protection, and power of God. He wasn't depressed because He didn't know God. Elijah knew God in a more personal way than many of us ever will. Elijah, devoted man of God that he was, was just depressed.

Devotion To God Doesn't Mean That We Won't Sometimes Feel Depressed.

Throughout Biblical history, we see evidence of God's people suffering from feelings of sadness, melancholy, fear, and angst. The Psalms are full of David's cries to the Lord. Jeremiah wasn't called the Weeping Prophet for nothing. Even Paul lamented the fact that three times he lifted up a specific request and three times God denied him. They were human; so are we. As such, we experience emotions and not only good emotions. We feel grief, anger, fear, and frustration. Couple that with physical exhaustion or mental confusion, and the resulting cocktail can be depression.

If you think I am over-estimating the extent of Elijah's feelings, look a little closer. After Elijah prayed to die, he slept, and he slept, and he slept until an angel woke him up and told him to eat. He did, and then, he slept some more until the angel woke him again. The angel told Elijah to eat and get strong for a journey, but Elijah didn't seem interested. He didn't even ask the angel or God where he was supposed to go. He just got up and took off, like a child who didn't get his way.

"Well, God obviously isn't going to take my life. So, I guess I will just do what I want, go where I want. He isn't listening to me anyway."

If you've read the story, you know that the trip turned into a wonderful blessing. However, Elijah obviously didn't wind up where God wanted him to go because in verse 9, after Elijah arrived at Mount Sinai, God asked him, "What are you doing here, Elijah?"

Elijah gave God his "woe is me" speech, and then God came to him—not in the strong wind, not in the earthquake, and not in the fire. God came to Elijah like a parent to a scared child. It's as if He bent down next to him and whispered, "What are you doing here, Elijah?" Like a boy still frightened of monsters, Elijah said, "They've killed all your people, God. I'm the only one left, and they are trying to kill me too."

If you can't exactly relate to Elijah's fear, surely you can relate to his fatigue, his sense of loneliness, his overwhelming sense of despair.

God didn't correct Elijah. He didn't condemn him. He didn't even try to coerce him into feeling differently. God gave Elijah a new set of directions.

It took forty days (and nights) for Elijah to reach this mountain. Couldn't God have stopped him along the way? Couldn't God have yelled at Elijah and asked, "Where are you going?" before he got to that cave? Why did God wait until Elijah had traveled so far before He spoke? Why did God go through the whole wind, earthquake, fire thing before He gave Elijah a new set of directions?

Sometimes God Doesn't Speak Until We're Ready To Submit.

Elijah's second response, though technically the same as his first, came at a point of submission. God told Elijah where he needed to go, where he would have gone first had he waited for God's instructions, and what he needed to do. While He didn't explicitly point out the error of Elijah's thought process, He did mention the 7,000 others in Israel who had also never bowed down to Baal. He made sure Elijah understood that he had never been alone.

Then, God answered Elijah's initial prayer. No, God didn't allow Elijah to die, but God did tell Elijah to anoint Elisha as his replacement. God knew that Elijah was finished, but God wasn't quite finished with Elijah just yet.

Elijah didn't argue, mope, or ask for another nap. The fact that he got up and went is evidence.

God Can Still Move Us Even When We Aren't Motivated.

So, Elijah backtracked to where he needed to be, did what God asked him to do, and found who God wanted him to find. Did that mean that he felt "all better"? Do you think that he was just bubbling over with excitement about the road ahead? The Bible doesn't say, but knowing human nature, I guess that wasn't the case. Elijah doesn't exactly seem like a bubbly kind of guy anyway.

The circumstances surrounding Elijah's discouraging feelings had not really changed, not yet anyway. He was still a hunted man. His life was still in danger, and, although God gave him a helper, it took time for his partner to become a friend. The truth is this—

External Peace Is Sometimes Elusive, Even For God's People.

We must understand what a life of faith is and what it isn't. It's not about always getting our way. It's not about always feeling good. A life of faith isn't necessarily one of ease on this earth. A life of faith, like Elijah's, is a life of reliance on God for provision, a reliance on God for protection, and a reliance on God for peace.

Peace, like joy, can be elusive, especially when life is lonely, when times are hard, and when rest seems too far away. Sometimes it seems like God doesn't hear us, that He doesn't care. It feels as if the storms are going to blow us away, like we are falling through the broken ground beneath our feet, or that we are being consumed by the flames of this life. Like Elijah, we have to remember. God is with us; He is listening; He is working, and He will speak. We just have to listen closely and rely on Him.

Notes:

September Week Four

Relying on God for Posterity

Read: 2 Kings 2:1-15

Primary Point: The best legacy we can leave is a life of faith.

Memory Verse: "Elijah was as human as we are, and yet when he prayed earnestly that no rain would fall, none fell for three and a half years!" *James 5:17*

Relying on God for Posterity

Elijah wanted to die. He thought he was all alone. He asked God to take his life, but God responded by telling him that he was one among many and by sending him a friend. Eventually, God answered Elijah's prayer. He didn't let Elijah die, but He removed him from this earth.
In this final story of Elijah's life, let's consider a few more lessons we can learn about living a life of faith.

Faithfulness To God Results In A Spiritual Family.

In our last lesson, we saw how God sent Elijah to commission Elisha and how Elisha accepted the call (1 Kings 19:19-21). Elisha became Elijah's successor. From this passage in 2 Kings, we can assume that they also became friends.

Some scholars estimate that as many as twelve years passed between their first meeting and the day that God decided to take Elijah to Heaven. Regardless of the time frame, the relationship between the two men had grown. Elisha, at least, had developed a distinct sense of loyalty to his friend, not wanting to discuss the upcoming departure but refusing to not be present when it occurred.

From all Biblical accounts, Elijah seemed to live a very solitary life. We know little of his history, and there is no record of any immediate family. It is very likely that Elijah did not have a wife or any children of his own. In his final hours on this earth, we are reminded of a great truth about living a life of faith. Elijah left behind a heritage of faith, not only in Elisha, but in the prophets and other believers from Bethel and Jericho and other areas where Elijah served. Regardless of our biological connections, a life of faithfulness will result in a spiritual family.

The Best Legacy We Can Leave Is A Life Of Faith.

When the time finally came for Elijah to be taken to Heaven, an audience gathered. At least fifty men watched, but only one got a front-row seat. As Elijah and Elisha prepared to say, "See you later," Elijah presented his friend with a request. "What can I do for you?"

Truthfully, Elijah had already given Elisha everything he could. Elijah had demonstrated for his friend a lifetime of obedience to the God they both served. So, when Elisha asked to inherit a double portion of Elijah's spirit and to become Elijah's successor, the request wasn't really one Elijah could fulfill. Since any power Elijah had was not from himself but from God, only God could give Elisha more.

If Our Motives Are Pure, God May Grant Great Requests.

At first glance, Elisha's request seems selfish. It almost seems grandiose. Think about the miracles God worked through Elijah. God made the rain to stop and to start again at Elijah's word. He lit the fire of the altar and won the battle with the prophets of Baal on Mount Carmel. Through the life of Elijah, God provided food for the hungry and brought the dead to life. Elisha was requesting that he wanted twice as much of whatever allowed Elijah to do those things. Elisha wanted to be twice as powerful as his friend, or that's the way it sounds.

I'm not sure that's really what was going on. The Bible says that Elisha requested a "double share" of Elijah's spirit. Since we know that Elijah was a man of God who only did what he did through the power of the Lord, it seems more likely that Elisha was actually requesting a double portion of the Lord Himself. How do we know this? Because God answered and gave it to him.

Sometimes, we ask great things, and God says, "no." Sometimes God doesn't give us what we want because He knows that what we want isn't what's best for us or someone else. Sometimes God doesn't give us what we want because He knows we are asking with the wrong motives. Sometimes, however, when our motives are pure, God may grant our great requests. Such was the case of Elisha.

The work of faith and obedience that Elijah began was continued through his successor, Elisha. It wasn't really about Elisha. It was about God. By granting Elisha's great request, more people witnessed the power of the Lord, more people were called to repent of their sins, more people came to know God. When our motives are aligned with God's, God may grant our great requests.

Our Faith Should Be Evident To Everyone Around Us.

Elisha's first miraculous act was an imitation. He struck the water and called out to God. It was if he were saying, "OK, God, are you going to give me what I asked for?" Only God, not Elijah, could have given him that power. The nearby prophets didn't miss the moment.

It was a risky move on Elisha's part. After all, Elijah made no promises. There was no guarantee that God would give him the power and authority on earth to do the same kinds of miracles his successor had done. Think about it. Moments before,

Elisha had been in distress, watching his friend be taken away in a fiery chariot. As he got up from the ground and picked up the cloak Elijah had left behind, he could have shuffled along the riverside, kicking pebbles, and pretending to talk to himself. He could have quietly prayed, "God, did you answer me? Do I have the same kind of power that you granted to Elijah? Will I be able to do the kinds of things he did?" He could have waited until the audience dispersed before he tested the waters, to see if God would really part them as He had before.

Instead, Elisha, walked boldly to the river, and called out loudly. He drew the attention of the audience who was busy launching a search and rescue party for Elijah. He didn't whisper. He didn't wait. Elisha knew that a life of faith should be evident to everyone. If God was going to say no to Elisha, it would be a public "no." Elisha's faith was in the one true God, and, whatever, the result, Elisha wasn't keeping any secrets. Elisha, like Elijah, was living a life of faith, the kind of life God wants us to live as well, a life lived in reliance upon God.

Notes:

October

Famous Falls of the Bible

October Week One

What We Learn from the Boy Who Fell Out of the Window

Read: Acts 20:7-12

Primary Point: Some circumstances are out of our control—trust Jesus!

Memory Verse: "You can make many plans, but the Lord's purpose will prevail." *Proverbs 19:21*

What We Learn from the Boy Who Fell Out of the Window

There is a little story tucked into the book of Acts that fascinates me. Jesus died, resurrected, and returned to Heaven. Paul was traveling and teaching, and the followers of Christ, now known as Christians, were growing in number and in faith.

One Sunday, the church gathered to celebrate the Lord's supper together. They most likely met in someone's home. There, in an upstairs room, with smoky, flickering lamps, Paul preached to a group of believers who sat, stood, and perhaps even laid about the room listening. A young man named Eutychus sat on the window sill where he could escape the stuffiness of the crowd.

Paul, who was leaving the next day, was determined to make the most of this opportunity and preached well into the evening. Sometime around midnight, his sermon was interrupted by a scream and then gasps as people jumped from their places of rest and ran towards the window. Eutychus dozed off and fell three stories. It was evident to the crowd that he was dead.

They ran outside; friends and relatives were beside themselves with grief. Paul pushed his way forward and bent over Eutychus. He lifted Eutychus in his arms and said the most unusual thing, "Don't worry. He's alive!" They all went back upstairs and continued to worship. We can only imagine the increased vigor in their service. I'm sure everyone was wide awake and listening. They shared the Lord's Supper together, and Paul continued preaching for several more hours.

It's no accident that God included this odd little story in His Word. So, what exactly are we supposed to surmise from it? Here are a few thoughts.

Bad Things Happen Even When We Are Doing Our Best.

Eutychus's name means "fortunate." Isn't that interesting? I doubt that he felt very fortunate as he woke up head over heels tumbling from the window that night. We don't know how old he was. I always picture him as a preteen or young teenager. Most likely with his family, he was at church on a Sunday evening, listening to a rather long-winded preacher. By all accounts, Eutychus was, on this night anyway, doing his best to be a "good" Christian. Being "good" didn't prevent something very bad from happening.

John 16:33 says in part, "Here on earth you will have many trials and sorrows." Contrary to the beliefs of some, Jesus did not promise us an easy life. In fact, if Jesus Himself, who lived a perfect, sinless life, suffered on this earth, what makes us so arrogant as to think that we won't?

We live in a sinful, broken world with other sinful, broken people. It is inevitable that bad things will happen to us, even when we are doing our best to live a Christ-like life. Being a Christian does not prevent us from hardship, sorrow, or grief. Even in hardship, though, God will never leave us or fail us. (Deuteronomy 31:6-8 and Hebrews 13:6)

Some Circumstances Are Beyond Our Control.

It seemed obvious to the crowd at the window that Eutychus was dead. He dropped "three stories to his death below." Of course, we don't have the EMT report. No ambulance came peeling into the church parking lot that night. The Bible doesn't even give us a graphic report of what he looked like there on the ground below.

Did his head hit first? Were there bones protruding through his arms from where he tried to break the fall? Was there a lot of blood? Is it possible that he simply knocked himself out? Maybe he didn't die after all. We really don't know.

It's interesting to me that the Bible doesn't report anyone praying, but I am confident that someone was. Among the gawkers at the window or the ones who ran down to get a better look, among the family members crying out, or the mothers shielding the eyes of their littles, I am sure there was someone praying, "Oh, Jesus, help Eutychus. Please, Lord, don't let him be dead. Please, Lord, touch and heal him. Help him get up and walk away from this."

Paul was the first responder. He bent over Eutychus and took Eutychus into his arms. Very little time seemed to pass before Paul shouted the good news. One second Paul was preaching, and the next he was running down the steps to check on the person who had fallen out the window.

While Eutychus was in Paul's arms, the life of Eutychus was not in Paul's hands. Only God could have saved Eutychus, and God did. Whether Eutychus died on impact and was resurrected or whether he just appeared dead, he miraculously walked away from a fall that could have killed him.

In Psalm 31, the psalmist reminds us that his life and our lives are in God's hands. Proverbs 19:21 reminds us that we can make many plans, but it's the Lord's purpose that will prevail.

We have to face the fact that often what happens or doesn't happen in our lives is out of our control. Thankfully, nothing is impossible for God.

Even After Something Life-Changing, Life Goes On.

The final few verses of this story seem so anticlimactic. Basically, everyone just went on about their business. They ate together. Paul kept on preaching, and then, sometime after dawn, he left. At some point, Eutychus was taken home, not just alive but also "well."

We can assume that everyone was relieved because Eutychus was OK, but we have to wonder if they weren't also relieved that the service had finally ended. Just think. We complain if the sermon lasts more than an hour!

It's a good reminder. Even after something life-changing, life goes on. Paul finished the sermon and went on his way. Since it was a Monday when they dismissed, people probably went to work just like they had the Friday before. Maybe some of them (surely Eutychus) went to bed first.

Being Saved Gives Us A Story.

Imagine the story that Eutychus had to tell! Imagine the things his mother or father must have talked about around the dinner table the next day or the next week. Imagine the children who were present that evening as they played in the streets the next afternoon. What would they have said?

"Did you hear about Eutychus? He fell from a third-story window! We thought he was dead, but God miraculously saved him! Look at him! He's just fine."

Maybe this little story is here just for those reasons, to remind us. Bad things will happen, even when we are trying to do our best, and sometimes, there is nothing we can do about it. Some circumstances are just out of our control, and regardless, life still goes on. Perhaps most of all, it's to help us remember that we, like Eutychus, have also experienced God's love and saving grace. We too have a story worth sharing.

Notes:

October Week Two

What Falling Walls Can Teach Us About Faith

Read: Joshua 6:1-20

Primary Point: God promises triumph in His time, but we must obey.

Memory Verse: "Faith shows the reality of what we hope for; it is the evidence of things we cannot see." *Hebrews 11:1*

What Falling Walls Can Teach Us About Faith

If you spent any time in church as a child, you have likely heard the Bible story around which our lesson is centered today—The Battle of Jericho. With God's miraculous intervention, the Israelites escaped slavery in Egypt but were condemned to wander in the desert for 40 years because of their disobedience to the Lord. Moses and all of that generation had passed away. Now Joshua was leading God's people into the Promised Land, and Jericho stood in the way.

Jericho was a city of several thousand people surrounded by two different walls that together would have appeared close to 10-stories high. To the Israelites, penetrating the city would have seemed impossible and, humanly, would have been so. For God, however, nothing is impossible. He gave Joshua a set of almost ludicrous battle instructions. He didn't call for battering rams to break down the barricades. He didn't ask for warrior wall climbers to scale the parapet and open the gate from the inside. He didn't even ask for the best archers to take aim against the guards of Jericho. God gave Joshua a plan that involved a lot of walking and a little yelling. In the process, He left us with a few powerful lessons on obedience.

Submission Often Precedes The Supernatural.

Joshua had a choice to make. He could believe God and obey the instructions that were given to him, no matter how ridiculous they seemed, or he could do things his way. The Israelites could have made the same mistake as they had years earlier. They could have chosen to not believe. They could have disobeyed. They could have tried to do things their own way, but they didn't.

Their obedience was a demonstration of faith, of trust. It was their way of acknowledging that God was in control, not them. When they obeyed, God responded with a supernatural display of His power.

What would have happened if the Israelites had not followed God's instructions? We don't know for sure, but instead of walking around the walls for seven days, I think they may have wound up walking around the desert for another 40 years. It makes me wonder how often we forfeit an opportunity to see God respond in supernatural ways simply because we choose not to submit to His will and obey His commands.

Obedience Isn't Effortless.

Obedience starts with an attitude of submission, but it doesn't end there. The Israelites had to get up and move. Simply agreeing with God about what had to be done wouldn't have been enough.

In addition, they were commanded not to talk. Can't you imagine the guards of Jericho taunting, jeering, and poking fun of the Israelites? They may have thrown things at them, spit on them, or shot arrows at them. Whatever happened, the Israelites could only march in silence. There could be no retaliation, no self-defense.

To us, looking back on the event, it may seem that the Israelites had the easy part of the job. After all, taking down the walls was the hard part, and God did that for them. Sometimes, though, what may seem easy at the onset actually isn't easy at all. All those warriors probably hated marching in silence. They would have given anything to "help" God out by shooting a few arrows at those guards. The priests may have been itching to set down the ark and offer God a sacrifice or pray a special prayer. Even the women and children may have had difficulty being obedient, wanting instead to hide away in the safety of camp.

Obedience begins with an attitude but definitely requires action and effort. It is not easy, and, in fact, may be hard. This is what makes obedience the truest expression of trust.

Triumph Comes With Time.

The first time around the walls was probably a novelty. There was new scenery to view. The second and third times, the Israelites may have been full of daydreams about what was behind those walls, what was to come. Surely, by the fourth and fifth days the trips had gotten monotonous. What about after that sixth time around on that seventh day? There must have been a sense of anticipation, of course, but also fatigue, maybe even a little frustration. Why did it have to take so long?

If you have ever faced a wall in your life, then you probably understand. Maybe you have tried to be submissive. Maybe you have done everything you know to act in obedience. Still, you are waiting, waiting for God to break down the wall that is holding you back from the victorious life He promised. It's a difficult place to be, wanting so badly to take matters into your own hands or being tempted to throw in the towel all together.

As Christ-followers we are guaranteed ultimate victory, but sometimes that victory takes a very long time. In fact, like Abraham and other patriarchs who "died still believing what

God had promised them." (Hebrews 11:13a), sometimes our triumph won't fully come until eternity.

The story of Jericho isn't just a fairy tale meant to inspire little ones to remember God's power. It's a real-life experience meant to remind us about the importance of obedience and how that obedience is a direct reflection of our faith. No matter how impossible the task seems, God calls us to listen to His instruction, obey His commands, and wait on His timing to bring the victory.

Notes:

October Week Three

What Happened When the Ax Fell in the Water

Read: 2 Kings 6:1-7

Primary Point: How we react in a moment of loss says a lot about who we rely upon.

Memory Verse: "Then call on me when you are in trouble, and I will rescue you, and you will give me glory." *Psalm 50:15*

What Happened When the Ax Fell in the Water

Years ago, Bro. Matt Lemster preached a sermon from 2 Kings 6:1-7. Despite having been a Christian for most of my life, having been in church all of my life, and being a frequent Bible reader, this was a Bible story I never remembered hearing before. Since that sermon years ago, I have only heard this passage preached upon one other time. The story is about a floating ax head.

The story opens with a group of prophets whose number had grown so large that they needed a new meeting space. Someone suggested that they get creative and build their own. So, they all packed up and went down to the Jordan River to cut some logs. Not long after arriving, mid-swing, an ax head from one of the men's axes flew off its handle and landed in the river. Obviously, ax heads are heavy. So, it immediately disappeared into the murky water.

If this happened to one of us, we would jump in the car and drive to the nearest Lowes or Home Depot to purchase a new ax. For the prophet, there were a couple of things that made this more devastating. First, in this time period, tools weren't nearly as inexpensive or easy to obtain, especially for a poor prophet. Second, this particular tool was borrowed.

If you ever borrowed anything of value, you can probably relate to this poor man's feelings. He was understandably upset.

Here he was trying to do a good thing. He was giving up his time in back-breaking work to help build a place of worship. Why would God allow such a frustrating thing to happen to him? If someone was going to have bad "luck" why couldn't it be lazy bones Bob who was hiding away behind the trees taking a nap?

It's human nature to think that if we are doing what God wants (or at least trying our best) then bad things shouldn't happen to us. Like the commercial says, "That's not the way this works. That's not the way any of this works."

Matthew 5:45 reminds us that the sun shines on evil people as well as the good, and rain falls on good people as well as bad. As a result of sin, we don't live in a perfect world. Just because we are Christians doesn't mean we are immune to bad things.

We Can Be In The Right Place, At The Right Time, Doing The Right Thing, And Things May Still Go Wrong.

So, the ax head flew into the air and splashed into the nearby river. I am sure for a split second the wood cutter was in shock. Then, what did he do? Did he jump in and try to retrieve it? Did he start stomping and whining about his bad luck? Did he wipe his hands and say, "Oh well, I guess my work is done for the day"?

No, he went to the one who could help, the one who had a place of prominence among this group—Elisha. The prophets knew enough to invite him on the trip. This prophet knew enough to call on Elisha when his ax head took flight.

What do we do when trouble comes our way? Do we kick, scream, and cuss? Do we jump in and try to fix the problem on our own? Or do we call upon the One who can do something about it.

In Psalm 50:15 God says, "Then call on me when you are in trouble, and I will rescue you, and you will give me glory."

How We React In The Moment Of Loss Says A Lot About Who We Rely Upon.

God wants us to turn to Him when bad things happen. His response may not always look like we anticipated, but He promises that He will rescue us.

When the dismayed prophet came to Elisha, Elisha had him point out the spot where the ax head had fallen into the river. Then Elisha threw a stick into the water, and the ax head floated to the surface. Obviously, this was a miracle. There was nothing particularly special about the stick, nothing magical about the water, nothing even amazing about Elisha. God caused that ax head to float.

Elisha then told the prophet to "grab it." Now think about this. If God could cause the ax head to float in the water, why didn't He just have it float right on over to the prophet. Why didn't it just pop itself back onto the handle? Would it have been that much harder, that much greater of a miracle?

Instead, the prophet had to go and get it. He not only had to walk over to the Jordan River, he probably had to wade in a little. He had to reach down and pick up that ax head, take it back up on the bank, and reattach it to the shaft (hopefully securing it a little better than before).

If you look throughout the Bible, some of God's most amazing miracles involved the work of God's people. God parted the Red Sea so the Israelites could walk across; He could have just transported them there. Naaman had to wash in the Jordan River in order to be healed of his leprosy; God could have healed him on the spot. In the New Testament, at Jesus's command the lepers were cleansed as they went to see the priests; He could have just said the word.

If the prophet never waded into the Jordan to retrieve the ax head, it would have either floated there until someone did, or it would have sunk again. In order for him to get the benefit of using the ax, the prophet had to pick up the ax head. There is no question. God doesn't <u>need</u> our assistance to perform miracles, but He often asks us to have a little skin in the game.

Complete Restoration Is Often Dependent On How Well We Receive It.

There you have it, three valuable lessons from one unusual Bible story. I firmly believe that every word in the Bible has been put there for a reason. God didn't include filler. God is trying to teach us, trying to convey a message in each story. I am so thankful for pastors like Matt Lemster and Tim Harris who introduced me to the story of the floating ax head and piqued my interest in all the other, obscure little stories throughout the Bible.

Notes:

October Week Four

What We Can Learn When a False god Falls Down

Read: 1 Samuel 5:1-5

Primary Point: God not only deserves our worship; He demands to be worshipped.

Memory Verse: "For the Scriptures say, 'As surely as I live,' says the Lord, 'every knee will bend to me, and every tongue will declare allegiance to God.'" *Romans 14:11*

What We Can Learn When a False god Falls Down

Anyone who has seen the movie Raiders of the Lost Ark, with Harrison Ford starring as the adventurous archaeologist Indiana Jones, knows a little bit about the Ark of the Lord (also known as the Ark of the Covenant). The Ark of the Lord was the holiest relic of Israel.
Every inch of its craftsmanship had been determined by detailed instructions from God. Inside the Ark were hidden the Ten Commandments, a pot of manna, and (Moses's brother) Aaron's rod.

Before the coming of Jesus and the indwelling of the Holy Spirit in believers, the Ark, which was housed in the Tabernacle (or later temple), was to be God's dwelling place on earth, the place in which God met with specially chosen representatives of mankind. Today's scripture passage tells of a time when the Ark had fallen into the enemies' hands.

The Philistines captured the Ark of the Covenant. This was a devastating blow to God's people since it would have literally felt as if God's presence had been lost. Equally, it was a tremendous boon for the Philistines.

Willing to admit that it housed a "god," they may have thought it would bring them some sort of good luck or fortune. Therefore, they judiciously treated it with as much respect as worshipers of a foreign god could. They placed it in their temple, next to their idol of the half-man, half-fish god named Dagon.

The people returned the next day to visit the temple, and there they found Dagon on his face before the Ark of the Covenant. Dagon didn't have legs. Images of how the god is believed to have appeared show a curving tail with the torso, head and arms of a man. His bottom half would have basically been a rocker. Have you ever tried to flip a rocker completely over? It isn't an easy task. Yet, somehow Dagon found himself face down in front of the Ark of the Lord.

The people sat the idol back up and went about their business. The next day, however, things got a little more dramatic. The idol of Dagon had fallen again, but only his torso remained in front of the Ark. His head and hands had been broken off and were in the doorway of the temple. Dagon had fallen, and he wasn't going to get up.

The rules and regulations surrounding the Ark of the Covenant were severe. If you watch the last scene in the *Raiders of the Lost Ark* movie (I usually close my eyes), you will have some idea. Everything about the Ark was holy, and God took it very, very seriously. Guidelines defined how it was to be created, what should go in it, how it should be carried, who was allowed to touch it, and when it was to be moved. Breaking these rules resulted in death. (Want an example? Read about Uzzah in 2 Samuel 6:1-7).

Why then, in the enemy camp, did God not just wipe out everyone who came in contact with the Ark?

Keep reading through 1 Samuel 5 and 6, and you will discover that things eventually did get really bad, bad enough that the Philistines returned the Ark along with gifts of gold as an offering. Although He could have, God did not just kill all of the Philistines as a result of their disrespect.

God Was Demonstrating His Compassion.

God did not hold these foreigners to the same level of accountability that He held His people. After all, they truly didn't know better. They didn't know Who He was or what the rules about the Ark were. Instead, He tried to make it evident to them that they were in over their heads, that they were dealing with Someone much greater than a statue. He tried to make Himself known to them. When we are tempted to think of God as being unkind, unmerciful, unbending, this lesson is a good example of how wrong we are.

Did the Philistines get rid of Dagon and immediately start worshiping the Lord as a result of this encounter? No, there is no indication that ever happened. However, I like to believe that somewhere among that group of people there may have been at least one person who heard the news of Dagon's fall and got it. I like to think someone understood the significance and said, "Wow, the god we serve fell on his face in front of the God of the Israelites. The God of the Israelites must be a powerful God, a truer God, than Dagon. I want to serve that God."

Romans 14:11 says, "'As surely as I live,' says the Lord, 'every knee will bend to me, and every tongue will declare allegiance to God.'" It is inevitable. Idol or not, Dagon didn't have a choice, and neither will we.

Every Knee Will Bow. Every Tongue Will Confess. One Day, Everyone Will Be A Believer.

Our God is the One true God, the creator of the heavens and the earth, the redeemer of our sins. God loves us, and He has provided a way for us to have a relationship with Him. God wants us to willingly choose to serve and worship Him.

If we don't do it now, we will in eternity. Then, we will know Who He is and will give Him the adoration that He deserves, but we will also be forced to face the consequences of our choices here on earth.

When the Philistines, rejoicing in their victory, brought the Ark of the Covenant into Dagon's temple and plopped it down right beside the idol of this merman, I'm not sure what they expected would happen. What took place reinforces (in my mind at least) that God definitely has a sense of humor. It's a comical story, but it is also a story that should give us pause for thought.

God Is A Compassionate God Who Not Only Deserves To Be But Also Demands To Be Worshiped.

Notes:

November

A Life of Gratitude, More than Just Thanks

November Week One

Thoughts and Thankfulness

Read: Colossians 3:1-17

Primary Point: When we think about the right things, we're more likely to be thankful.

Memory Verse: "Since you have been raised to new life with Christ, set your sights on the realities of heaven, where Christ sits in the place of honor at God's right hand. Think about the things of heaven, not the things of earth." *Colossians 3:1-2*

Thoughts and Thankfulness

A life of gratitude goes beyond simply saying "thank you" to others or even to God. A thankful heart originates from a thankful life. To demonstrate true thanksgiving, we must have the proper attitude, but unfortunately this doesn't come easy or naturally for many of us.

So, this month we are going to dig into Colossians 3:1-17 to learn more about how we can foster a thankful spirit. Each week, our primary passage will be the same, but I will explore the verses in smaller sections as we work through the month. Let's try to find out what this passage has to say to us and how we can apply those principles to our lives.

First, let's get a little background. Colossians was a letter written by the apostle Paul to the church in Colossae, a city in Asia Minor. Paul, who had most likely never been to this church, wrote the letter while in prison in Rome, around the year of AD 60. In this lesson, we are going to specifically look at what Paul has to say in verses 1-4.

A long time ago, country music star, Kenny Rogers, sang *The Greatest*. If you have never heard it, look it up on YouTube. It tells the story of a little boy playing baseball by himself. He bragged of his hitting prowess and then threw the ball up in the air with every intention of knocking it out of the park. Three times he swung, and three times he missed. After the third strike, anyone listening to the song feels for the boy, knowing he must surely feel disheartened. Instead, the small ball player cheerfully admits that he never realized he was such a great pitcher.

This story illustrates a concept that is integral to living a life of gratitude. Just like the little boy switched his train of thought, we too can switch ours. By adjusting what we think about and the way we think, we can regulate whether or not we live a life of gratitude.

In Colossians 3:1-4, we are given two specific commands. We are told to set our sights on the realities of Heaven and to think about things of Heaven, not the things of Earth. What do you think these commands have to do with thankfulness?

What really matters, or what really should matter to us, should be the same things that matter to God. Our perspective should be a Godly perspective, not an earthly perspective, an eternal perspective, not a temporal one. If our real lives are with Christ in Heaven, it makes sense that we should think about Christ and Heaven as much, if not more, than our current lives.

Ultimately, of course, Heaven is a better place because that is where God is, and we know that in Heaven everything will be right and good. There will be no more sin, no more sorrow, and no more pain. Colossians 3:4 also alludes to the fact that there will be rewards in Heaven for those who serve Christ (as we share in His glory). By thinking of our future reward in Heaven and life with Christ Himself, we can be grateful for our salvation and look forward to our eternal home with Him. We have this hope regardless of our current circumstances.

The second command in these verses indicates that we should be thinking about Heavenly _things_ rather than earthly things. By exploring Philippians 4:8 we can discover what the Bible says are some specific things on which we should think.

"Finally, brothers and sisters, whatever is _true_, whatever is _noble_, whatever is _right_, whatever is _pure_, whatever is _lovely_, whatever is _admirable_—if anything is _excellent_ or _praiseworthy_—think about such things."

These are the kinds of thoughts that help lead us towards a life of gratitude.

The little boy in the Kenny Rogers' song chose to switch his train of thought. Instead of focusing on his less-than-stellar batting abilities, he chose instead to focus on his pitching skills. We too have a choice in what we think.

Pastor Tim Harris once said, "If you are going to be like Christ, you have to think like Christ." Thinking about earthly things will often bring us down and cause us dissatisfaction and grief. Thoughts of Heaven and Heavenly things provide peace, hope, and love. Thinking about Heaven can help us focus on and prioritize our everyday lives. As we look at life through the eyes of God, we should begin to understand the futility of much of what we are striving for and, instead, seek what He wants. We can learn to live with more of an eternal perspective and be more content with what we have been given. So, let's remember that a life of gratitude begins with thinking about the right things.

Notes:

November Week Two

Learning to be Content

Read: Colossians 3:1-17

Primary Point: When we think about and thank God for what we have, we're less likely to complain about what we don't.

Memory Verse: "Put on your new nature, and be renewed as you learn to know your Creator and become like him." *Colossians 3:10*

Learning to Be Content

This month we are studying Colossians 3:1-17 to learn more about what it means to live a life of gratitude. Last week, we were reminded that by switching our train of thought from earthly things to Heavenly things, we can begin to look at our lives from an eternal perspective, think about things that please God, and look forward to our future in Heaven, regardless of the circumstances that we are facing here on earth. These types of thoughts help us to rely upon Christ for present help and give us hope for a future in Heaven with Him.

This week, we are going to look at another way in which we can learn to live a more grateful life. Let's first learn a little more about the church to whom Paul originally wrote this letter.

Colossae was a city that was on the trade route from Ephesus to the Euphrates River. Although almost completely forgotten in Roman history, it was probably a very important city at one time. Because of the fertile land, it was a great place to raise sheep and was famous for its red-dyed wool. Because it was a trade city, the citizens would have been exposed to a variety of visitors with a variety of beliefs. This may be the reason that doctrinal falsehoods began to creep into this primarily Gentile church. Paul wrote this letter to make sure that certain truths were known and understood.

Basically, Paul wanted all believers to know that since Christ is Lord of all creation, He most certainly should be Lord of our lives. Contentment demonstrates that God is reigning in our lives.

Of course, discontentment is not always sinful. We should be discontent with sin. We should be discontent when we see sorrow or hurting. We should be discontent when we find flaws within ourselves or see areas that need improvement. Discontentment, like every other attitude or action, becomes sinful when it is a reflection of desires that stray outside of God's Word or God's will for us, when we are "I centered" instead of "God centered."

That type of sinful discontentment hinders a life of gratitude because many sins are a byproduct. For example, sexual immorality, impurity, lust and evil desires (listed in verse 5) are a result of not being content with God's definition of sexual purity and marriage. Greed is obviously not being content with what we have. Sins such as anger and rage (and the others listed in verse 8) are often a result of not being satisfied with the way in which something is being handled or a certain circumstance. Just like Lucifer was discontent with his position and Eve was discontent with her status, sin often originates with discontentment. Basically, sin is often a result of not being content with the type of life that God has given us or that He wants us to live.

God is our provider. He is the giver of all the good things we have in our lives. When we are discontent, we are failing to be thankful. When we act out sinfully as a result of our discontentment, we are like a spoiled child throwing a tantrum. Instead of being content, we demand or try to take what we want regardless of whether it is His will.

Obviously, that's not God's plan for us and not God's best for us. God wants us to get rid of these sins and to find contentment in Him and His Word. Interestingly enough, while contentment leads to gratitude, gratitude actually can help us be more content. The more intentionally thankful we are, the more unlikely that we will be discontent. When we begin to think about and thank God for what we have, we are less likely to complain about what we don't. When we choose to rebuke the sins in our lives that are a result of or contribute to discontentment, we are taking another step closer to a life of gratitude.

Charlie Brown once said, "What if today we were just grateful for everything?"[7] By remembering to be thankful for even the everyday small blessings, we can help foster a spirit of contentment and gratitude in our lives.

This doesn't happen by accident. We need to practice thanksgiving. Since gratitude and contentment go hand-in-hand, we have to be intentional with these efforts. When we have a concern, a need, even a want, we need to take them to the Lord in prayer.

Just like thinking about Heaven helps us to realign our wants with God's wants, learning to be content helps us to remember how much good God has already given us.

Notes:

November Week Three

Treating Others Well

Read: Colossians 3:1-17

Primary Point: Gratitude involves generosity and leads us to be people who generally treat others well.

Memory Verse: "Above all, clothe yourselves with love, which binds us all together in perfect harmony." *Colossians 3:14*

Treating Others Well

This month we are studying Colossians 3:1-17 to learn more about what it means to live a life of gratitude. In our studies thus far, we have been reminded that by switching our train of thought from earthly things to Heavenly things, we can begin to look at our lives from an eternal perspective, think about things that please God, and look forward to our future in Heaven regardless of the circumstances that we are facing here on earth.

We have also learned that gratitude and contentment go hand-in-hand and that a lack of gratitude can lead to sinful actions. Discontentment spurs us to take our blessings for granted and to pursue things that are not in our best interest. When we give up sinful actions that either result from or lead to discontentment, we are actually opening our hands to receive and enjoy the blessings God has for us.

Thankfulness both results from and breeds contentment. Thinking the right thoughts and learning to be content help us to rely upon Christ more for our present help and our future hope, thereby helping us to live life with more gratitude.

In this week's lesson, we will continue our study by examining Colossians 3:10-15.

Gratitude includes being thankful. It also means being appreciative and kind. Even though most everyone would agree with this definition, we have to admit that it is in our human nature to be sinful and selfish, not to be grateful.

Paul tells us that as Christians we have a new nature. We should be different. He points out that this is a process because we are being renewed. Then, he gives us specific commands as to what we can do to generate this new character. He tells us that we are to be tenderhearted, merciful, kind, humble, gentle, and patient. He tells us that we should make allowance for each other's faults and to forgive each other.

It has been said that selfishness is the surest way to misery. The Bible is full of scriptures that tell us to love each other, to be kind, to forgive, and to look after one another. Paul reminds us that there is a connection between gratitude, love, and peace. The Bible makes it clear that how we treat others is a reflection of our relationship with Him. Gratitude is a decision to **act** not necessarily feel. For most of us, this does not come naturally, therefore, it must be intentional.

When we treat others with love, compassion, humility, and kindness, we are demonstrating that our identity is not rooted in what we have, but to Whom we belong. Gratitude should lead us to be a people who are loving, generous, and kind —a type of people who generally treat others well.

Everyone wants to see the world changed for the better, but too often none of us want to perform the small acts of kindness that will make a difference. Living a life of gratitude results from thinking the right kinds of thoughts, means learning to be content with what we have, and involves treating others well. How can you show gratitude this week in the way you interact with the people in your life?

Notes:

November Week Four

More than Just Saying Thanks

Read: Colossians 3:1-17

Primary Point: A life of gratitude results from filling our lives with Christ.

Memory Verse: "And whatever you do or say, do it as a representative of the Lord Jesus, giving thanks through him to God the Father." *Colossians 3:17*

More than Just Saying Thanks

This month we have been studying Colossians 3:1-17 to learn more about what it means to live a life of gratitude. We have been reminded that a life of gratitude begins with thinking about Heavenly things rather than earthly things. We should learn to be content and avoid sins that result from discontentment, and we should treat others well. Gratitude is a decision to act not necessarily just something we feel. Therefore, we have to be intentional about cultivating gratitude in our lives.

This week, we are going to conclude our studies by examining Colossians 3:1-17, but first, let me begin with a story.

Jimmy and Johnny were constantly getting into trouble, and their parents were at a loss on how to discipline them. Whenever anything bad happened in their neighborhood, everyone knew that the two brothers were most likely involved. Not knowing what else to do, the parents finally asked their pastor if he would have a word with the boys. The pastor agreed but asked to see them individually.

Jimmy met with the pastor first. Upon arrival, the little boy sat in the big chair across from the pastor's desk. The pastor leaned across the desk, looked the little boy straight in the eyes, and said, "Son, where do you think Jesus is?" Jimmy just looked at him.

The pastor tried again, leaning closer to the boy and speaking a little louder, "Jimmy, I asked you a question. Where do you think Jesus is?" The little boy still did not respond. The pastor was growing a bit frustrated at the boy's insolence, but he was determined to start a dialogue with him.

So, he took a deep breath and in his deepest, loudest, hellfire-and-brimstone preaching voice, boomed, "Where is Jesus?"

At that, the youngster jumped out of the seat, scurried out the door and ran all the way home where he quickly hid in his bedroom closet. Johnny found him and anxiously asked, "How was it? What did the pastor say?"

Jimmy shivered slightly and said, "Johnny, we're in real trouble now. Jesus has gone missing, and they think we did it!"

Where is Jesus? How would we answer that question? In the first verse of this series, Paul tells us that Christ is sitting in the place of honor at God's right hand. In verse 16, he reminds us that Christ should actually fill our lives.

Remember, Paul is writing this book to believers—those who have agreed with Christ that they are sinners, have confessed their sins and asked forgiveness, and have trusted in Christ for salvation. If you have given your life to Christ, then Christ lives in you through the power of the Holy Spirit. Paul wrote this letter to remind believers about the facts of their faith and encourage them with specific ways that they can live to please Christ. We have been applying these particular scriptures to how we can live lives of gratitude.

In the latter portion of the passage, Paul tells believers to teach and counsel each other, sing psalms, hymns, and spiritual songs, and to be representatives of Christ. These may be things that you generally associate with a church service, but Paul doesn't specifically mention a service here.

Instead, he is actually describing ways that we worship, and he is encouraging us to do these things individually every day. These things should be part of our lives, not just our Sunday morning-going-to-church-lives, but every day. At home, at work, at school, at the ball games, in the store, on vacation, every single day, the gospel message should be part of our lives, because we are representatives of Christ.

In addition, Paul points out that all these things should be done with a thankful heart. Worship is actually an outpouring of our thankfulness to Christ. All our blessings come from God. Therefore, gratitude isn't just saying thanks; it is honoring God in our everyday lives. It's appreciating what He has done, what He is doing, and what He will do.

When we are truly tuned into Christ and what He has done for us, our lives will be filled with worship, and we will desire to reflect Christ in an accurate way to the lost world around us.

Contrary to what little Jimmy thought, Jesus isn't missing. He lives in Heaven with God the Father, but He also lives inside Christians through the presence of the Holy Spirit. All of this comes full circle, starting with Jesus and ending with Jesus. Through Jesus, we can think the right thoughts, learn to be content, and treat others well, but we need to remember that a life of gratitude ultimately results from filling our lives with Christ. When we do that, we can represent Christ well and give thanks to God the Father. In fact, we can go beyond just saying thanks; through Jesus, we can truly live a life of gratitude.

Notes:

December

Considering the Lives of the Christmas Characters

December Week One

How to Find Favor When the News is Unfavorable (Mary)

Read: Luke 1:26-38

Primary Point: Our submission should not depend on our state of affairs.

Memory Verse: "For the word of God will never fail." *Luke 1:37*

How to Find Favor When the News Is Unfavorable (Mary)

Have you ever received unexpected news? Maybe you found out that you were losing your job. Maybe your doctor called with a bad diagnosis. Maybe you discovered that your spouse betrayed you. Maybe you learned that you have to move again. Maybe, like me, you received the call that a loved one died. We all know how it feels. It's like having the rug pulled out from under us. It leaves us dizzy, disoriented, and dangerously close to a fall.

So, just imagine how Mary felt. She was a young, virtuous woman, living a rather ordinary life, and she was engaged to be married. In her culture, that meant that the arrangement was already sealed. All that was left was the consummation. While love was not necessarily a requirement for marriage, we can assume that Mary looked forward to being a wife and that she looked forward to the day she would have a family of her own. Then, she received the strangest message. She was going to be a mom after all, but not in the way that she—or anyone else—expected.

Mary was understandably stunned. After all, she may not have been a worldly woman, but she knew enough of the birds and the bees to understand that this wasn't possible. She knew what she had and had not done! She knew what everyone would think. While we look back on the angel's message in celebration, to Mary this would not necessarily have appeared like good news, especially not at first.

Mary's Response Offers An Example For All Of Us To Follow When We Receive Unwelcome News.

First, **Mary asked a question**. Questioning a divine message might seem like a mistake to you. However, Mary wasn't being disrespectful; she was genuinely curious. She had just been told that she was going to have a baby, and she knew that was not physically possible. So, Mary wasn't afraid to ask an honest question. We don't have to be either. God already knows our confusion, our frustration, our fears, even our anger. Why shouldn't we converse with Him about how we are feeling? 1 Peter 5:7 says that we should "cast our fears on Him." Philippians 4:6 tells us to "pray about everything." God wants to hear from us. So, just like Mary, don't hesitate to ask Him those questions that are swimming around in your head. Talk to God about what is happening.

After Mary asked the question, **she listened to the answer**. Of course, she couldn't have truly understood the answer she received. Mary had never even been with a man, but she knew that a woman needed a man to get pregnant, right? Mary's pregnancy, however, was going to be different; this was going to be BIG; this was going to be something only God could do. God was telling her something important, but Mary had to listen to hear the message. John 8:47 reminds us that "anyone who belongs to God listens gladly to the words of God." Romans 10:17 tells us that "faith comes from hearing." Like Mary, at some point we have to stop asking questions and actually listen to what God has to say.

Mary also responded with a submissive heart. Even when we ask the questions, even when we listen carefully, sometimes God's answers just won't make sense. Regardless, James 4:7 and 1 Peter 5:6 remind us to humble ourselves under God's authority. Submission is not dependent upon our state of affairs. Sometimes, like Mary, we just have to take it all by faith. Mary didn't argue with God. She didn't try to reason her way out of what was happening. She didn't request an alternate plan. Mary submitted. She accepted God's authority and yielded to His will. She said, "OK, Lord. Whatever you want." It's the same response God expects from us.

So, learn from Mary's example, and plan now how you will handle difficult news. If it hasn't already, it's sure to come your way.

- **Converse with God.**
- **Commit to Listen, and**
- **Concede to His will.**

Who knows how your story might end? Remember, what seemed to be a "not-so-good" message for Mary turned out to be the beginning of the Gospel story—the greatest news the world has ever heard. Mary found favor with the Lord, and we can too—even when the circumstances seem unfavorable.

Notes:

December Week Two

How to React When Our Plans are Revised (Joseph)

Read: Matthew 1:18-24

Primary Point: If we are wise, we will seek and know the truth of God's Word.

Memory Verse: "Teach me your ways, O Lord, that I may live according to your truth! Grant me purity of heart, so that I may honor you." *Psalm 86:11*

How to React When Your Plans are Revised (Joseph)

Sometimes our best laid plans go awry. Joseph and Mary had plans, big plans. They were engaged. During this time in Biblical history, this engagement was really more important than the wedding ceremony itself, which was a mere formality. For all intents and purposes, Mary and Joseph were legally and morally bound to one another. Their families had worked it all out. Most likely, a mohar (the bridal price) had already been given by Joseph or his family to Mary's family. Mary's dowry, what she was taking into the marriage, had been determined. Her bags were packed. Wedding bells were about to ring.

God, however, had a different plan. To Joseph and Mary, this unexpected pregnancy must have seemed like a nightmare. In fact, the appearance of infidelity would have been such a breach of morality that Joseph could have legally petitioned for Mary to be stoned. At the very least he could have chosen to publicly humiliate her. Joseph, being a righteous man, formulated a new plan. Life had taken a turn for the worst, but he would manage. Of course, the wedding would be cancelled. There was no way to get around that, but he didn't want to bring any more shame or harm to Mary than she had already brought upon herself. It was a tough decision, but he decided to handle the matter more discreetly. He would avoid the public eye as much as possible.

Do you wonder what Joseph may have been thinking about as his eyes closed and he slipped into sleep that evening? Was he still mourning the life he had just lost, the dreams that he believed would never come true? Had he resigned himself to the facts, believing that he had come up with the most suitable option to handle this sticky situation? Perhaps, he was praying that God would heal his broken heart and provide him with a new bride-to-be. Whatever was on his mind that late night so long ago, we know this. God was getting ready to throw another wrench in Joseph's plans. Joseph's life was about to be redirected, again.

It happens in our lives as well. Things can be going along just fine when, all of a sudden, here comes a curveball. Sometimes we recover well. We pick ourselves back up and take another swing, only to get knocked back down again. Joseph's response serves as an example for how we should react when God revises our stories.

Joseph Recognized The Truth.

To you and I this message would have seemed unbelievable, but Joseph didn't argue because he had heard the prophecies. He was, like all of the Jewish people, awaiting a Savior, and while he may not have understood the details, his role in the plan, or any of the implications for his life, he definitely recognized the Word of God. Knowing the truth helped him believe it.

Where do we find truth? How do we know truth? In John 14:6, Jesus says, "I am the way, the truth, and the life." In John 17:17, Jesus, while praying to the Father on behalf of His followers, asked God to "Make them holy by your truth; teach them your word, which is truth." If we want to effectively deal with the unplanned detours of our lives, like Joseph, we must be able to recognize the truth.

To do that, we have to first know Jesus, and then, we must know God's Word.

Most people would agree that the best way to prepare for an exam is to study a little bit over the course of several days or weeks. "Cramming" is not usually an effective means of learning and retaining information. While we can certainly be introduced to Jesus and begin to learn about God's Word in moments of crisis, confusion, or collapse, it is always more helpful to prepare in advance. <u>Remember, in order to recognize the Truth, you have to know the Truth.</u>

Joseph Obeyed.

When Joseph woke up after having come face-to-face with God's direction, he didn't rethink the situation, reconsider his plans, or redirect his mind. He didn't bow down and begin to pray again, didn't make a visit to the local rabbi for clarification, didn't go talk it out with his parents or Mary's family. He did what he was told; he followed through with the wedding. He became Mary's husband.

James 1:22 tells us that we shouldn't just hear God's Word; we should also obey it. 2 John 1:6 reminds us that if we love God, we will do what He commands. If we claim to know and love the Lord and wish to receive His approval and blessings on our lives, then <u>we have to react in obedience</u>—even when things don't work out the way we anticipated or wanted.

Proverbs 16:9 says, "We can make our plans, but the Lord determines our steps." Sometimes, God takes us on a path we never would have chosen for ourselves. I am sure that Joseph never dreamed that he would have the privilege of raising the Savior. It wasn't the plan that he had for his life, and it wasn't necessarily an easy road to travel, but he was blessed and honored as a result of his obedient heart.

When our lives take unexpected turns, what should we do? If we are wise, we will seek and know the truth of God's Word, and then we will obey. It's the beginning of the Christmas story. It was for Joseph, and it is for us as well.

Notes:

December Week Three

What God Expects After You Encounter Immanuel (Shepherds)

Read: Luke 2:8-20

Primary Point: When we have an encounter with God, we must share it with the world.

Memory Verse: "Publish his glorious deeds among the nations. Tell everyone about the amazing things he does." *Psalm 96:3*

What God Expects After You Encounter Immanuel

They were ordinary people doing ordinary things, just like you and me. I seriously doubt that they had any inclination that night would be any different than any other. Maybe they were gathered around a campfire laughing and eating a bite of dinner. Perhaps some had already dozed off after spending the day chasing sheep from one green hillside to the other. There were probably one or two patrolling the perimeters keeping an eye out for predators hungry for mutton. They were shepherds, doing what shepherds do, when they received the unexpected news that led to a revision of their evening plans and an encounter they would never forget.

Sometimes it's interesting to look at what the Bible doesn't say as well as what it does say. Notice that the passage doesn't really say much about the encounter with Christ. We get the angel's message in detail (7 lengthy verses), but we get very little about what happened when they got to the manger (only 1 verse). As important as it must have been, when God inspired Luke to write these verses, He chose not to camp on the primary experience. Instead, we are given a great narrative about what came before and what happened after the shepherds met Christ.

We all know the before. We've watched the angelic visitation reenacted in churches and auditoriums, on television specials, and on the pages of comic strips. We've heard their proclamations from bathrobe-clad children and famous actors, and we've sung their story in carols, choirs, and along with the radio in the car. What we rarely discuss is what happened to the shepherds after that famous meeting.

Verse 17 says that after seeing Jesus, "the shepherds told everyone what had happened and what the angel had said to them about this child." The shepherds weren't concerned that they were smelly from having been in the fields with sheep for days on end. It didn't matter that they were tired from a sleepless night. Of course, they knew what people thought of them. They were uneducated and considered uncouth, but they didn't worry about what the citizens of Bethlehem thought. They didn't consider whether they would be rejected, humiliated, or made fun of. In fact, they gave little thought at all to how their audience would respond or react. They just told people—all the people—everyone, anyone—about what had happened. They knew that their experience was so great, so beautiful, so important, so unique, that they couldn't keep it a secret.

I like to imagine the shepherds heading back to their fields, weaving through the crowded streets of Bethlehem, waving down friends and family who were surprised to see them within the city limits, shouting, "You are NEVER going to believe what happened to us last night!" I can just picture them bumping into disgusted strangers or responding to the merchants' calls. "Let us tell _you_ about where we've been!" Can't you just see them stopping weary travelers to tell them the good news? "We HAVE to tell you who we met."

In Psalm 96:3 God reminds us that we should do the same. If we have encountered Christ, our enthusiasm should be no less than that of the shepherds. We should be exuberant from our experience, so much so that we, like Peter and John, proclaim, "We cannot stop telling about everything we have seen and heard." (Acts 4:20) So, why don't we? Do we think the gospel story is any less sensational than the story the shepherds shared? Are we more concerned about less trivial matters like how we will be perceived among our peers? God expected the shepherds to share their encounter with Jesus; He expects no less from us.

Eventually, the shepherds made their way back to the fields. They went back to their flocks, back to their "day jobs," back to the lonely hillsides outside Bethlehem. These were the first earthly beings outside of Mary and Joseph to have met the Savior, but they didn't head off to Samaria as foreign missionaries. They didn't join the shepherd-to-priest training program at the local temple. They didn't even volunteer to lead the praise team at the next Bethlehem revival. They went back to what they knew; they were shepherds.

As they watched their sheep eating peacefully, the sun warming their tired faces, they could have taken turns napping or started preparing the mid-day meal. They could have set aside their experience as a great memory, something to regale the campfire crowd and traveling visitors. The Bible tells us that even though they went back, they did so "glorifying and praising God for all they had heard and seen."

Not everyone is called to a "special" ministry. Many of us, after having met Jesus, will go back to the ordinary. Like the shepherds, we may be ordinary people doing ordinary things, but we will be different. We should be changed, and, therefore, praise and worship must be a natural outcome of an encounter with Christ. Psalm 100 commands us to "worship the Lord with gladness." Romans 15 11 says to "Praise him, all you people of the earth." Hebrews 13:5 says that we should offer "a continual sacrifice of praise to God, proclaiming our allegiance to his name."

One night long ago, in a faraway place, ordinary men had the privilege of meeting God's own son, Immanuel.

What did God expect from them after such an extraordinary encounter? The same thing He expects from you and I—our praise and worship and public proclamation of His glory.

Notes:

December Week Four

What to Do When You're Looking for Answers (Wisemen)

Read: Matthew 2:1-12

Primary Point: Discerning God's will starts by studying His Word.

Memory Verse: "Work hard so you can present yourself to God and receive his approval. Be a good worker, one who does not need to be ashamed and who correctly explains the word of truth." *2 Timothy 2:15*

What to Do When You Are Looking for Answers (Wisemen)

We all have questions. Sometimes our questions are about little things.

- *What should I wear today?*
- *Where should I eat lunch?*
- *Should I get a dog or a cat?*

Sometimes our questions are really important.

- *What major should I choose in college?*
- *What kind of career should I pursue?*
- *Who should I marry?*

Sometimes our questions are heart-changing.

- *What is my purpose in life?*
- *Is God real?*
- *If so, does He really care about me?*

The wise men, just like scientists today, made a career out of asking questions, and it was one very important question that landed them smack dab in the middle of the Christmas story. They had been studying their favorite subject—stars—when they saw a special star rise in the night sky, a star that foretold the birth of a king. Somehow, they understood that this baby king was an extremely important person, a person so important that He was worth a long trip, worth expensive gifts, worthy even of their worship. They didn't know the name of this King; they didn't know what country He would govern, and most importantly, they didn't know how to find Him. From their search, we can learn much about what we should and shouldn't do when we seek answers to the questions of our hearts.

Be Careful Where You Seek Answers.

While the Bible doesn't explicitly say so, we assume that the wise men not only saw the star rising in the east but also followed it to Jerusalem. That's where they made a pit stop. We don't know why. Perhaps they stopped over for a bite to eat and a good night's rest at the local Holiday Inn. Perhaps they got impatient with the slow progress of their trip. Perhaps they saw the castle as they were taking a detour through town and conjectured that maybe the *new* king was actually the *son* of the *old* king. Whatever the reason, they got the bright idea to ask King Herod, a notoriously wicked and paranoid ruler, where the newborn King could be found. To say that King Herod was "deeply disturbed" was probably an understatement.

Of course, the answer they eventually received was correct. The leading priests and religious teachers pointed the wise men in the direction of Bethlehem, and Herod politely asked them to report back when they found the baby. Truthfully, they never really needed to ask. The star took them to the destination.

Sometimes, when we are seeking answers, we are like the wise men. We look in all the wrong places. While there may be times to talk to trusted advisors, picking up the phone to call our mother, our spouse, or our best friend, isn't the first thing we should do. Consulting a psychic, reading the horoscope, glancing at an almanac, or reading the best self-help books won't give us the answers we need. James 1:5 tells us, "<u>If you</u>

need wisdom, ask our generous God, and He will give it to you." Ephesians 5:10 tells us to "carefully determine what pleases the Lord." Proverbs 3:5-6 says, "Trust in the Lord with all your heart; do not depend on your own understanding. Seek His will in all you do, and He will show you which path to take."

When we have heart questions, we need to remember that our first and greatest resource is God Himself. He speaks to believers through His indwelling Spirit and through His Word. 2 Timothy 3:16-17 says," All Scripture is inspired by God and is useful to teach us what is true and to make us realize what is wrong in our lives...God uses it to prepare and equip His people to do every good work."

The star that the wise men originally saw, that had most likely guided them all the way to Jerusalem, kept guiding them right to Jesus. They never needed Herod or anyone else. God gave them exactly what they needed, and He promises to do the same for us as well.

Be Prepared To Follow Wherever God Leads.

After meeting Jesus, the wise men may have felt their quest was over, but they still needed to get home. When it was time to leave, God didn't use a star to guide them. He used a dream to warn them not to return the same way they had come and to avoid another visit with King Herod. It was an unexpected turn of events, but they didn't dismiss it as indigestion. They went home by another route.

It does us very little good to seek God's answers to our questions if we fail to follow where He leads. How do we follow? We start with obedience to the simple commands of His Word.

Isaiah 48:17 says, "I am the Lord your God, who teaches you what is good for you and leads you along the paths you should follow." Ephesians 5:1 says, "Imitate God, therefore, in everything you do, because you are His dear children."

Discerning God's will is not always an easy task; however, it starts by studying His Word and obeying His commands. Someone once said that the problem is not that we, as Christians, don't understand the Bible. The problem is most often that we don't obey the parts we do understand.

So, if you are seeking answers to the heart-questions of your life, go to the Lord Himself. Take your questions to Him in prayer, and listen to His voice through the Holy Spirit and His Word. Obey what you know He wants you to do, and trust that He will guide you to the next step. Remember, the closer we draw to God, the more easily we will hear and know His voice, and the more readily we will discern the paths He is leading us to take.

Notes:

December Week Five

What to Do When You Can't Go Back

Read: Matthew 2:13-21

Primary Point: God's greatest promise is His own presence.

Memory Verse: "This is my command—be strong and courageous! Do not be afraid or discouraged. For the Lord your God is with you wherever you go." *Joshua 1:9*

What to Do When You Can't Go Back

In the classic story, The Wizard of Oz, Dorothy clicks her heels and wishfully recites, "There's no place like home; there's no place like home." Despite having a series of adventures and making several new friends in Oz, she realized that home is where the heart is, and she wanted to go back. Do you wonder if Mary and Joseph felt that way? After all, Bethlehem was supposed to be an excursion, not a relocation.

After receiving the government summons, the couple completed the difficult trip, experienced the hardship of birth, wondered at their interesting visitors, and yet, they had still not gone home. Jesus was circumcised and named at eight days old. Then, around 40 days after birth, a purification offering was given for him, as was the custom for first-born sons. Since the Bible refers to Jesus as a child and says that the family was living in a house (no mention of a manger) when the wisemen visited, we know that more time had elapsed. Because of Herod's edict to kill boys under two, many scholars speculate that Jesus was around the age of two. We can't know for certain, but we can positively say that this was more than a weekend visit. Months, if not years, passed, and the little family was still in Bethlehem.

After the wisemen left, God warned Joseph not to go home but to go instead to Egypt to escape the wicked King Herod. Had Mary and Joseph already been planning their trip home to

Nazareth? Had they packed their bags and planned their trip well before the wisemen graced their door? Were they secretly worried that their family and friends would still be judgmental about the circumstances of Mary's pregnancy, or were they anticipating a joyful reunion with the new grandparents? Whatever they were thinking, whatever they were feeling, the Lord made it clear to Joseph. They couldn't go back.

What about you? Have you ever wanted to go back? Back to a place of happy memories, back to a time when things seemed better, back to a particular day or a particular moment to relive something good or to redo a mistake? While we may be able to revisit a location, we can never go back in time. So, what can we learn from Mary and Joseph's trip to Egypt that will help us when our heart aches to go back?

Look For God's Provision

Regardless of the era or culture in which you live, one thing is always the same. Everyone needs some form of income in order to survive. Have you ever wondered how Mary and Joseph lived in Egypt? Of course, Joseph was a carpenter, and he may have been able to find employment in that trade, but it's obvious that God provided in another way as well. He sent the wisemen to present gifts befitting a king, one of which was gold. It is very likely that Joseph and Mary used that gold to help sustain them during their stay in Egypt.

Paul wrote in Philippians 4:19, "And this same God who takes care of me will supply all your needs from his glorious riches, which have been given to us in Christ Jesus." In Matthew chapter 6, we are reminded that if God cares enough to take care of the birds and lilies, He will surely take care of us. Sometimes we want to go back because we are afraid of what lays ahead, but if God has called you to something (or away from something), He will provide.

Believe In God's Promises

Even when we experience God's provision, we can get homesick. Don't you think that Mary and Joseph were? After all, Egypt wasn't prime real estate for the Jews. The Israelites remembered well their ancestral enslavement to the Egyptians; it wouldn't have been first pick for a vacation home. In addition, the close family connections that were valued in their culture would indicate that Mary and Joseph probably had family members in Nazareth whom they loved and missed. Even if their physical needs were being provided for, we have to wonder how they coped with the emotional longing to be in a familiar place with those they loved.

Many of us can relate. Sometimes, like Mary and Joseph, we are separated from family and friends because of distance. Other times, death has snatched them from our arms. How do we cope with the overwhelming ache of separation? The same way the new parents did; they believed in God's promises. When God warned Joseph to flee to Egypt, He also told him to stay there "until I tell you to return." While they surely missed their families and friends, they could cope with the separation because they knew that it was temporary.

Trust In God's Plan

God has given us promises too. When we are aching to return to something to which God has called us from, when we are longing to be with someone God has called away, when we are craving to have something that God has put behind, we are assured that He knows, and He cares. In Matthew 28:20 Jesus says, "I am with you always," and in Hebrews 13:5, He promises, "I will never fail you. I will never abandon you." God's greatest promise to believers is His own presence. He loves us. He is with us, and if we seek out the promises that He provides in His Word, we will find assurance of His presence, His peace, and His comfort when we are longing for what has been left behind.

When life often takes us on unexpected and even painful detours, we can rest in God's provision, His promises, and His plan. Sometimes, like Mary and Joseph, we have to go to "Egypt," but Egypt is never our final destination. Eventually, God always brings His followers home.

Notes:

The Romans Road to Salvation

We Are All Sinners.

"As the Scriptures say, 'No one is righteous —not even one.'" *Romans 3:10*

"For everyone has sinned; we all fall short of God's glorious standard." *Romans 3:23*

God Provided A Means Of Salvation.

"But God showed his great love for us by sending Christ to die for us while we were still sinners." *Romans 5:8*

We Can Know That We Are Saved.

"If you openly declare that Jesus is Lord and believe in your heart that God raised him from the dead, you will be saved." *Romans 10:9*

"For everyone who calls on the name of the Lord will be saved." *Romans 10:13*

A Personal Note

If you don't know Jesus today, then I encourage you to not wait. If you believe in Christ, then all you need to do is confess your sinfulness to Him and ask Him to forgive you. Turn your heart away from your own self-centeredness, and give your life to Christ. Once you make this decision, don't keep it a secret. Tell someone, and seek guidance from a local pastor or a fellow Christian on how to grow in your faith. Reach out to me at tricia.brown@thegirlsgettogether.com. I'd love to hear all about it.

Bibliography

1. "GDPR Support". *Ajc.Com*, 2020, https://www.ajc.com/news/national/billy-graham-quotes-made-christian-principles-accessible-millions/vmeaUI4HGTKhI9kdimpn9J/.

2. "8 Antisthenes Antisthenes Quotes From Successories Quote Database". *Successories.Com*, 2020, https://www.successories.com/iquote/author/39445/antisthenes-antisthenes-quotes/1.

3. Tripp, Paul. "You Talk To Yourself". *Paultripp.Com*, 2020, https://www.paultripp.com/wednesdays-word/posts/you-talk-to-yourself.

4. Lewis, CS. "The Great Divorce Quotes By C.S. Lewis". *Goodreads.Com*, 2020, https://www.goodreads.com/work/quotes/1215780-the-great-divorce. Accessed 6 Nov 2020.

5. Alcorn, Randy C. *Heaven*. 1st ed., Tyndale House Publishers, 2004.

6. "Nigeria: Released Hostage Reports That Leah Sharibu Is Alive And Well". *Csw.Org.Uk*, 2020, https://www.csw.org.uk/2020/01/20/press/4528/article.htm. Accessed 6 Nov 2020.

7. Schultz, Charles M. *Peanuts Cartoon*. 2020, https://i.pinimg.com/originals/50/4e/7f/504e7f4ac6433b9c7d53246f55f7a146.jpg. Accessed 7 Nov 2020.

Acknowledgements

Thank you, Ian, for loving and supporting me, for giving me the freedom to pursue this dream, and for giving me a beautiful office, a place to shut the door and dream.

Thank you, Sjon-Paul, for using my own words against me and for encouraging me to do hard things.

Thank you, Braxton and Ryan, for being patient with me when I shooed you out of my office and for loving me even when I'm grumpy.

Thank you, Brandon, for being my staunch defender and for sharing my creative spirit. I miss you and look forward to seeing the artwork you're creating for our home in Heaven.

Thank you, Mom and Dad, for raising me to know Truth and for giving me all the tools to pursue it. Thank you for cheering me on and believing in me when I didn't believe in myself.

Thank you, Marsha and Nancy, for holding me up when I couldn't hold myself and helping me laugh again.

Thank you, Shannon Tuggle, Teresa McEwen, BJ Cummings, Amanda Turner, and Reyna Anderson for your love, friendship, and support.

Thank you, Cherman Keown, for being my biggest fan.

Thank you, Patti Sawyer for proofreading this manuscript, and **Pastor Tim Harris** for reviewing this manuscript for theological errors.

Thank you to everyone who loved, supported, and prayed for me, especially during the past two years. You have been God's hands and feet in my life, and I will never forget.

About The Author

Tricia K. Brown

Tricia K. Brown is daughter of Gerald and Jean Carter; the wife of Robert Ian Brown; and the mother of Sjon-Paul (Lauren), Brandon, Ryan, and Braxton. As a child living in Westmoreland, Tennessee, Tricia accepted the Lord as her Savior during bedtime prayers with her mom. She graduated from Western Kentucky University with a BA in English and Print Journalism and currently lives in Bowling Green, Kentucky. Tricia has been a homeschool mom and freelance writer and editor for than twenty-five years. In 2018, after the unexpected death of her 20-year-old son, Brandon, she founded The Girls Get Together. Through this ministry, Tricia shares stories of life, loss, and laughter to encourage women to grow in their relationships with the Lord and each other. In her free time, she loves to take long baths, read, watch superhero movies with her sons, and fellowship with friends and family. Her greatest desire is to know and love the Lord and to love others well.

Connect with Tricia K. Brown

The Girls Get Together
Tricia K. Brown
Bowling Green, Kentucky

Email Tricia at tricia.brown@thegirlsgettogether.com

Follow ThisGirlTriciaB on Twitter and Instagram.

Connect with Tricia and The Girls Get Together
on Facebook and YouTube.

Visit thegirlsgettogether.com to sign up for Tricia's free weekly email devotional and to find out more about The Girls Get Together minstry.

Made in the USA
Columbia, SC
10 December 2020